GOING TO THE CHAPEL
PLANNER

To: Pam
You are going
to be the most
radiant bride in 2004.
Love,
Janilla

Also by The Editors of *Signature Bride* Magazine

Going to the Chapel

Going to the CHAPEL PLANNER

The Editors of Signature Bride Magazine

Produced by The Philip Lief Group, Inc.

BERKLEY BOOKS, NEW YORK

This book is an original publication of The Berkley Publishing Group.

GOING TO THE CHAPEL PLANNER

A Berkley Book / published by arrangement with
The Philip Lief Group

PRINTING HISTORY
Berkley trade paperback edition / December 1999

The Penguin Putnam Inc. World Wide Web site address is http://www.penguinputnam.com

ISBN: 0-425-17052-7

BERKLEY ®
BERKLEY BOOKS are published by The Berkley Publishing Group, a division of Penguin Putnam Inc.,
375 Hudson Street, New York, New York 10014.
BERKLEY and the "B" design are trademarks belonging to Penguin Putnam Inc.

PRINTED IN THE UNITED STATES OF AMERICA
10 9 8 7 6 5 4 3 2 1

Acknowledgments

A WARM THANK YOU to the many people who have been instrumental in the creation of this second book by the editors of *Signature Bride* magazine. Your vision, contributions, and dedication are greatly appreciated:

Boyega and Jonathon Adewumi of Nigerian Fabrics and Fashions
Lee Bradley of The Gold Connection
David Kelly Crow
The customer service staff of Invitations by Dawn™ mail-order catalog
Herbert Garrett of Garrett's Photography and Video
Geoffrey Conners of Geoffrey Conners Graphic Design
Stacy Jones of Pioneer Balloon Company
Shelley Bundy King of Carson Pirie Scott
Cindy Malin of the Greater Fort Lauderdale Convention and Visitors Bureau
Dabney Montgomery for his patient support of his wife as she worked on this book
Dr. Kwaku Ofori-Ansa
Reggie Payton
Barbara Pflaumer of Alfred Angelo
Tony Rose of Tony Rose Studios
Polly Schoonmaker of Polly's Cakes
Dorothy Shi
James Spada
Christine Valdes of Premier Resources, Inc.
Cookie Washington of Phenomenal Women Design
Elaine Young of Hopscotch Communications

The Project Team

Publisher
> Debra Kronowitz, *Signature Bride* magazine

Editorial Director
> Judy Linden

Project Manager
> Adrienne Ingrum

Writer
> Sarah Gearhart

Wedding Consultants
> Amelia Montgomery
> Linnyette Richardson-Hall

Illustrators
> Elaine Young of Hopscotch Communications
> Geoffrey Conners Graphic Design

Assistant Editor/Photo Researcher
> Fiona Hinton

Contributors

W E'D LIKE TO GRATEFULLY acknowledge and thank the writers whose articles, which first appeared in *Signature Bride* magazine, are now used in this book:

Andrea Diaz, "Wedding Consultants, Good, Bad and Ugly," January/February 1997.

Mary Jo Rasmussen, "Choosing a Honeymoon Getaway You'll Both Love," Spring/Summer 1995; "Tropical Paradise," January/February 1997; "Savor the Caribbean," Fall/Winter 1996.

Ata Rivers, "Paradise . . . the Sights, Tastes, and Sounds of the Caribbean," Fall 1997.

Contents

Dear Reader,

WE ARE PROUD to present to you the second book within our *Going to the Chapel* series. Our staff has designed this workbook to help you plan one of the most important days in your life.

We suggest you utilize it to its fullest extent. You'll be glad you did! We've designed it as a keepsake, so years down the road, you can pull it out, curl up on the couch, and lose yourself in your memories.

We understand that although this is a very special time in your life, it can also be a hectic and stressful one. Relax! Enjoy! We assure you, when you pull this book out after your wedding day, you will look back and smile!

As publisher and founder of *Signature Bride* magazine, I want to personally say "thank you" to everyone involved in this project. Our Special Contributing Editor Linnyette Richardson-Hall, The Philip Lief Group, and our own project team have done an outstanding job in creating the most comprehensive wedding workbook for you.

A special thanks to all the photographers, models, and writers, as well as the *Signature Bride* magazine staff, for your talents and dedication.

And last, but certainly not least, a big thank you to you, our reader, for supporting *Signature Bride* magazine and the *Going to the Chapel* series. You are the reason we are here and are going to stay here for a long, long time.

On behalf of myself and my staff, we wish you and your man a lifetime of love, happiness, and good times.

May God bless . . .
Debra Kronowitz

**The ultimate result of all your planning will be a day
overflowing with love and joy that celebrates *your* heritage *your* way.**

OU'RE ENGAGED! Congratulations and best wishes to both of you. You are about to embark upon the most important and exciting event in your life. Your engagement is your commitment to spending the rest of your lives together. Your wedding will be your rite of passage and your vows a proclamation to your family, friends, and community.

You are starting to ask yourself questions such as, "Where do we start?" "How do we go about getting everything done?" "Should we hire a wedding consultant/coordinator?"

"How much will it cost?" You're beginning to plan your dream wedding, envisioning your special day, and trying to figure out how to make it happen.

Remember, this is *your day*, and it should reflect *your dreams*. The dreams relatives and friends will have for your wedding are worth consideration, but keep your vision in mind. This is a time for self-expression like no other time. Decide now to be you, to have your wedding in your own style, your way.

This workbook is intended to serve you both as a planner and a keepsake. Used in conjunction with *Going to the Chapel*, it will see you through all the details of your engagement, ceremony, and postnuptial wrap-up. In the process of planning and executing this most special of days, you will enjoy lots of lovely thoughts, appreciate many simple moments when your relationships deepen, and discover precious bits and scraps of information of which memories are made. This workbook is a place where you will record them all, both for the practical purpose of ensuring that your wedding day comes off perfectly as you dreamed it and for the bonus of effortlessly creating a scrapbook. It will be a reminder in the years—even generations—to come of this sweet time when you planned the joining of your lives together.

Think of this book as your ultimate wedding consultant. Amelia Montgomery, of Weddings by Amelia, a New York–based bridal consultant service, and Linnyette Richardson-Hall, founder of the Association of Minority Wedding Professionals and Premiere Event Management, and Special Contributing Editor, *Signature Bride* magazine, have poured every bit of professional expertise they provide to clients into this workbook. While no book can replace the services of a professional wedding consultant, this book is designed to be your essential wedding planner if you're going it alone or working with a posse of family and friends.

If you're like most couples, you'll have lots of help in planning your wedding. Parents, friends, sorority sisters, frat brothers, other-mothers, relatives, and, of course, professional wedding consultants may all have a piece of your nuptial action plans. We at *Signature Bride* say, "It's all good, get others as involved as you wish." This workbook is even more useful in shared planning. Use the book as a couple if you're planning your Big Day together. (It's fun to contrast and compare his and her handwriting, and deciphering those illegible scrawls are great smooch ops.) Pass the book from hand to hand if yours is a team planning process. Your planner turns into a fun sort of signed yearbook of all those who helped make your day happen. And, if you're blessed to have a wedding consultant, this book will be that catchall record that will make communication and follow-up a breeze. Says Amelia, "Even clients for whom I handle every detail of their wedding preparations, I recommend they keep a notebook. Your wedding is the most important event of your life, and I try not to duplicate anyone else's wedding. I want the bride and groom to share their unique wishes with me, and getting them to write key things down is one of the best ways to do that."

So, whether you're the wedding general determined to keep all the orders straight or leaving the details to others, you'll be well served by this workbook. Our theme has been, "The divine is in the details." Our goal has been to make all the minute planning as enjoyable—well, almost—as the wedding day, and to leave you with a scrapbook that will hold as many memories as your honeymoon. OK, OK, but you really *will* want to hold onto it as a keepsake!

Let the planning begin. The workbook goes hand in glove with the chapters in *Going to the Chapel*. We suggest you read or at least skim through that entire book. That will give you an overview of the complete process leading up to and surrounding the Big Day. Then find your favorite writing instrument and proceed to chapter 1 of this planner.

One last word as you start: Do use the space provided and photocopy pages, work sheets, and lists, when necessary. It may at first feel like overkill, but trust us, you'll be glad you wrote it all down. If you're one of those sisters or brothers or even mothers who keeps it all in your head, believe us, you will *lose* your head before this thing is over. Write it down, honey! We're sure you've heard stories—and we've *seen* them!—where the limo forgot to pick up Grandma, or everyone thought everyone else had ordered the cake, or the bride read 6/9/99 delivery on the receipt for the wedding dress as June 9, plenty of time for the wedding—when the tailor wrote it meaning September 6. Details never seem important until they're overlooked. Use this planner and all its seemingly excessive forms and fill-in-the-blanks. We hope you'll never know why all this detail was so necessary, and we are sure that if you do use them, you'll enjoy your Big Day with the blessing of *calm*.

Happy wedding planning!

Linnyette Richardson-Hall
Special Contributing Editor to *Signature Bride* magazine

You are each other's dream come true.
We'll help you envision the day of your dreams and make it all become a reality.

One

CREATING A VISION OF YOUR DAY,

YOUR STYLE, YOUR WAY

S YOUR WEDDING DAY a year or just months away? Regardless of how much or how little time you have to plan, take a few minutes to sketch out your ultimate wedding scenario. If you and your fiancé each write down, in as much detail as possible, what you imagine your Big Day to be, you will have the basis for achieving a joint vision as well as the foundation for all the planning and preparations that will make your dream a reality. And you'll look back on these few scribbles as those first cherished plans of your life together.

T o help you get started, here are five different styles of weddings you can use as guidelines for creating your memorable day:

Afrocentric. An Afrocentric ceremony celebrates our African heritage by incorporating music, rituals, food, garments, and jewelry from the Motherland. You can add African touches to any style of wedding.

African-American. Rejoice in your own family traditions and the rich cultural heritage we have from both continents: our religious faith, our sense of community, our sumptuous cooking, our generous hospitality, and our music and dance.

"Traditional". The classic European wedding—all satin, lace, pearls, and tuxedos—is the fantasy many of us have had since childhood.

Destination/Honeymoon Wedding. You dream of being married in an exotic, faraway spot where you will also spend your honeymoon.

Progressive Wedding. You want to celebrate in several different locations, revisiting places that were important in your courtship and sharing your happiness with loved ones in a variety of towns, states, or even countries, who may not be able to travel to you.

Use these as starting points and then mix and match elements you like from each. Perhaps you have always seen yourself as a fairy-tale bride, resplendent in white lace, but you also want to honor traditions from the Motherland. It's your day. Envision a ceremony and celebration that will be meaningful for you.

Then jot down a detailed description of your vision below, including the location, the time of day and time of year, the style of the ceremony, what you'll be wearing, and how many attendants and guests you envision.

Each of you should work separately at first. No peeking or sharing! Put down your individual visions. Don't second-guess each other; that is, don't put down what you think your mate-to-be envisions. Each of you being true to yourself is the only way the two of you can begin to truly understand and consider each other's desires.

❧ *Your Dream Vision*

Bride's Vision

Location _____

Time of day _____

Time of year _____

Style of ceremony _____

Officiant(s) _____

Style of dress _____

Number of attendants _____

Number of guests _____

Special Features _____

_____

_____

_____

_____

Bridegroom's Vision

Location _____

Time of day _____

Time of year _____

Style of ceremony _____

Officiant(s) _____

Style of dress _____

Number of attendants _____

Number of guests _____

Special Features _____

_____

_____

_____

_____

_____

_____

_____

Compare scenarios. First exchange them and read them silently. Then, with your fiancé, take a careful look at the elements of each. If your visions are word-for-word the same, one of you is not being true to yourself. If you're like the vast majority of couples, you'll have some differences. Discuss ways to keep those at the heart of your joint vision, even if each of you will have to give up one or more of the your own wants. If you find that your individual visions are very different, which is also very common, begin with the elements that you have in common. Decide together on the elements that are most important to both of you and build a shared vision around them. Don't be surprised if this takes some time. You might even need to sleep on and revisit the discussion several times before you're both comfortable. Remember that loving respect for each other's differences and willingness to compromise are valuable qualities in a marriage. List the elements you agree on below.

❧ Your Joint Vision

Location _____

Time of day _____

Time of year _____

Style of ceremony _____

Officiant(s) _____

Style of dress _____

Number of attendants _____

Number of guests _____

Special Features _____

_____

_____

_____

_____

_____

Between now and your Big Day, a lot will happen. You'll expand on your joint vision. You'll do lots of planning. Likely, others will influence and help you in planning. But, you'll return again and again to these early pages. They are your wedding vision. Hold on to that imagined scene and let all you do make it a reality.

WEDDING CALENDAR

The following calendar is a master plan you can use as you organize and plan. Review it now and amend it—yes, mark it up!—to suit the time frame that applies to you. So, if you have three months to plan, you'll have to shorten the time line. If you have two years, you can s-t-r-e-t-c-h things out.

Congratulations again, and happy wedding planning.

Remember, the journey is as important as the destination.

Wedding Calendar

12 Months Before:

- ✓ Buy a wedding planner or date book.
- ✓ Determine budget with fiancé.
- ✓ Determine the date of the wedding.
- ✓ Choose the location for the ceremony and reception (make reservations).
- ✓ Determine style—Afrocentric/European-American (formal/informal)—and select colors (which can also be your theme).
- ✓ Select your attendants and ushers.
- ✓ Hire a wedding consultant (optional).
- Book photographer and videographer.
- Book musicians (if Afrocentric, dancers and drummers).
- Book florist.

9 Months Before:

- ✓ Make appointment to visit clergy or judge with fiancé.
- ✓ Begin development of guest lists: Four separate lists are prepared to determine who is invited. The bride, her parents, the bridegroom, and his parents each compile lists of relatives and friends without consulting each other.
- Select and order bridal gown, headpiece, and accessories.
- Register for wedding gifts with fiancé.
- Visit travel agent to make honeymoon plans.

6 Months Before:

- ❧ Hire a bakery chef.
- ❧ Book limousine service.
- ❧ Order invitations, announcements, and stationery.
- ❧ Hire caligrapher (optional).
- ❧ Complete honeymoon plans with travel agent.
- ❧ Select and order bridal attendants' dresses, headpieces, and accessories.
- ❧ Select bridegroom's wedding wear.
- ❧ Select bridegroom's attendants' wedding wear.
- ❧ Order wedding rings and engraving.

3 Months Before:

- ❧ Complete master guest list and start addressing invitation envelopes.
- ❧ Choose attendants' gifts.
- ❧ Plan recording and display of gifts.
- ❧ Reserve a block of rooms at a local hotel for out-of-town guests.
- ❧ Get a physical (although not a prerequisite in many states).
- ❧ Book hairdresser and discuss a particular hairstyle.
- ❧ Confirm with dress shop or seamstress the delivery date of gown.
- ❧ Select and purchase your trousseau.

6–8 Weeks Before:

- ❧ Mail invitations.
- ❧ Pick up wedding rings.
- ❧ Buy wedding gift for groom.

- Select and purchase attendant's gifts.
- Have final dress and bridal veil fitting.
- Sit for portrait.
- Send announcement to newspapers.
- Submit special request list to photographer and videographer.
- Submit special music list to band or DJ.
- Plan party for bridesmaids.
- As wedding gifts arrive, send Thank You notes.

2 Weeks Before:

- Get marriage license with fiancé.
- Finalize honeymoon reservations.
- Address wedding announcements for mailing on wedding day.
- Start packing and prepare going-away outfit.

1 Week Before:

- Give final count of guests to caterer.
- Purchase traveler's checks.
- Give bridesmaid's luncheon or party.
- Move clothing and other items to your new apartment (or house).
- Finalize details with florist, photographer/videographer, chauffeur, etc.
- Confirm rehearsal date and dinner details, which should take place 2 or 3 days before ceremony (allowing time for other last-minute details).
- Give attendants their gifts on rehearsal dinner night.

The romance, the ring, and the realization that you're going to spend the rest of your life with this wonderful person—these mark your engagement. As you plan your wedding, you'll get to know each other better and better. You'll learn each other's style of getting things done and discover even more ways you complement each other.

Two

WE'RE MAKING IT PERMANENT:

ANNOUNCING YOUR ENGAGEMENT

OU'RE GOING TO spend your lives together, and you've got a shared vision of how you'll formalize and celebrate that commitment. What a joy it is to share that news with the world. You'll be greeted by hugs, even tears, and with the great pride that the Black community bestows on those who are carrying on our traditions of sharing and building.

The way the two of you announce your engagement, both formally and informally, can strengthen your relationships with those closest to you and let the world know of the love and pride with which you take this momentous step. Family, friends, colleagues, and associates will all take their cues from the style and presentation of your announcement.

INFORMAL ANNOUNCEMENTS

Your heart will guide you in deciding whom to tell first: your parents, your children (if you have any), your other-mothers, and extended families will surely be at the top of your list. But don't second-guess yourself if your sister-friends and your fiancé's "brothers" are among the first you want to tell. Sometimes our chosen family is as close as our blood ties.

To avoid unintentionally overlooking someone special, follow your head as well as your heart by deciding in advance on the best order and the best circumstances for these most important announcements. The following checklist will help you keep track of those you want to tell personally.

❧ Checklist for Telling Family and Friends

NAME	NOTES	DATE TOLD

NAME	NOTES	DATE TOLD
_____	_____	_____
_____	_____	_____
_____	_____	_____
_____	_____	_____

You will probably need more space than we have provided, so photocopy these pages to continue your list.

FORMAL ANNOUNCEMENTS

Be sure you've told all your close family, friends, and associates before you make formal announcements so that no one special feels they were left to read about your great news in the weekly paper. Before you send your announcement to your local newspapers, purchase copies of each one you plan to contact. Write your announcement following their styles, and for help, use our work sheet. Note the days that the wedding announcements are published. Phone the newspapers to find out the lead time you will need to have your announcement appear on the date you wish, the name of the appropriate editor, and the type of photograph to send along with the announcement, if any. On the back of each photograph, tape a sheet of paper with a caption that includes your names and the photo credit (photographer's name). In most cases, the newspaper staff will not send the photographs back to you, so be sure you can spare them. If you and your fiancé are not from the same town, be sure an announcement is published in both hometowns.

Use the following work sheet to keep track of the newspapers to which you have submitted your announcements:

❧ *A Work Sheet for Submitting Newspaper Announcements*

Bride's Local Newspaper

Newspaper_____

Lifestyle editor (contact) _____

Phone_____

Deadline for copy _____Submitted _____Confirmed _____

Deadline for photo _____Submitted _____Confirmed _____

Groom's Local Newspaper

Newspaper_____

Lifestyle editor (contact) _____

Phone_____

Deadline for copy _____Submitted _____Confirmed _____

Deadline for photo _____Submitted _____Confirmed _____

Other Newspaper

Newspaper_____

Lifestyle editor (contact) _____

Phone _____

Deadline for copy _____Submitted _____Confirmed _____

Deadline for photo _____Submitted _____Confirmed _____

❧ *Announcement Information Checklist*

Here is a sample of the type of information most newspapers will ask you to submit for the engagement announcement.

Bride

Name _____

Education _____

Occupation _____

Father's name_____

Occupation _____

Residence _____

Mother's name _____

Occupation _____

Residence _____

Groom

Name _____

Education _____

Occupation _____

Father's name_____

Occupation _____

Residence _____

Mother's name _____

Occupation _____

Residence _____

Wedding date (time of year or month) _____

If you're not sure how to word your announcement, the following work sheet and sample wording will help you. If none suits your personality or style, sit down together and draft an announcement in the space provided. Remember, newspapers often have their own style and may not vary much from their usual wordings.

Newspaper Announcement Wording Work Sheet

_____

_____

_____

_____

_____

_____

_____

_____

_____

_____

_____

_____

_____

Sample Wordings for
Engagement Announcements

Traditional wording, announced by the parents of the bride:

Mr. and Mrs. Henry Palmer announce the engagement of their daughter, Nichole, to Gregory Driver, the son of Mr. and Mrs. George Driver of Hartford, Connecticut. Ms. Palmer, a summa cum laude graduate of Howard University, is a photojournalist in New York City for the Amsterdam News. Mr. Driver, who graduated cum laude from Vassar College and received his M.B.A. from New York University, is a systems analyst for AT&T, also in New York. An early autumn wedding is planned.

Note: If the parents of the bride don't live in the city where the announcement is being made, you'd also include their place of residence: e.g., if this announcement is published in a New York paper, you'd specify "Mr. and Mrs. Henry Palmer of Atlanta, Georgia."

If your parents are divorced, and neither has remarried:

Mrs. Olivia Palmer [or she may use her maiden name with her married name, "Mrs. Patterson Palmer"] *announces the engagement of her daughter, Nichole, to Gregory Driver. . . . Miss Palmer is also the daughter of Mr. Henry Palmer of Atlanta.*

Note: If your parents are still friendly, they may want to make the announcement jointly:

Mrs. Olivia Palmer of Chicago and Mr. Henry Palmer of Atlanta announce the engagement of their daughter, Nichole...

Otherwise, the one who raised you—usually your mother—does the honors.

If your mother has remarried:

Mr. and Mrs. Charles Greene [her new married name] announce the engagement of Mrs. Greene's daughter, Nichole Palmer.... Miss Palmer is also the daughter of Mr. Henry Palmer of Atlanta.

Note: Here the mother has chosen to announce the engagement with her new husband, with whom the bride may be especially close. It is also acceptable for both natural parents, even if remarried, to announce jointly:

Mrs. Charles Greene of Chicago and Mr. Henry Palmer of Atlanta announce the engagement of their daughter, Nichole Palmer...

If one of your parents is no longer living:

Mr. Henry Palmer announces the engagement of his daughter, Nichole, to Gregory Driver... Miss Palmer's late mother was the former Olivia Patterson....

(Note: This wording allows you to pay a special tribute to the deceased parent, perhaps mentioning his or her profession or special achievements.)

If both parents are no longer living:

You may ask a close relative or friend to make the announcement:

> *Mr. James Palmer announces the engagement of his niece, Nichole Palmer, to Gregory Driver. . . . Miss Palmer is the daughter of the late Mr. and Mrs. Henry Palmer.*

Or, if both your and your fiancé's parents are deceased, you may announce the engagement yourselves:

> *Nichole Palmer, a photojournalist, is to be married to Gregory Driver, a systems analyst for AT&T, in early autumn. Miss Palmer is the daughter of the late Mr. and Mrs. Henry Palmer of Atlanta. Mr. Driver is son of the late Mr. and Mrs. George Driver of Hartford, Connecticut.*

If you're remarrying:

> *Mr. and Mrs. Henry Palmer announce the engagement of their daughter, Nichole Palmer Parks* [if you kept the name of your previous husband] *to Gregory Driver. . . .*

Your fiancé can adapt these guidelines to the circumstances of his parents.

Place a clipping of your published announcement here.
Be sure to cut out the newspaper name and date.

Y ou will likely want to share your joyful news with your church, fraternity, sorority, and political and community organizations. Record them on the checklist below, noting the form of the announcement (spoken or written).

❧ Submissions Checklist

	ORGANIZATION	FORM OF ANNOUNCEMENT	DATE SUBMITTED	DATE ANNOUNCED
Bride				
Church/temple	_____	_____	_____	_____
Workplace	_____	_____	_____	_____
Other	_____	_____	_____	_____
Other	_____	_____	_____	_____
Groom				
Church/temple	_____	_____	_____	_____
Workplace	_____	_____	_____	_____
Other	_____	_____	_____	_____
Other	_____	_____	_____	_____

Chances are, someone will throw you an engagement party. Your good news is cause for celebration, so whether it's formal or informal, let others share your joy. You'll want to keep a record of this party, and your host might even ask you for your preferences in planning the bash.

Use this form for either purpose.

❧ *Engagement Party Work Sheet*

Hosts _____

Time _____

Date _____

Place _____

Additional wording on invitation _____

_____

_____

_____

(Style formal/informal) _____

_____

You'll also probably be asked for a guest list, so be ready. This list will help make sure no one is left out and make it easy for your host. Make photocopies if you need more space.

❧ *Engagement Party Guest List Work Sheet*

NAME	ADDRESS	PHONE

Be sure to keep track of the gifts you'll receive from the engagement party. And don't forget gifts of time and hospitality, as well as those who bring a dish or a bottle of something!

❧ *Engagement Gift Thank You Work Sheet*

NAME	ADDRESS	DATE NOTE SENT

Maybe you're already sporting a newly chosen stone your fiancé presented to you when he popped the question. Maybe you're still teary-eyed that you're the next generation to wear his grandmother's engagement ring. But if you're like lots of couples, you'll shop before you tie the knot. While you may hit your favorite malls and jewelry and department stores that offer ready-to-wear rings, you might want to consider hiring a jewelry designer to create a ring using symbols that have special meaning for you or to compose a ring using African symbols. The choices are as endless as the cultures of the Motherland—from the Adinkra images of West Africa to letters of the Swahili alphabet of East Africa. Use the work sheet opposite to keep track of the jewelers and designers you visit and to comparison shop. Record your final decision in the Purchasing checklist, so years from now, when these pages are cherished, yellowed refreshers to your memory, your grandkids will know the details of *their* heirloom ring.

African-inspired engagement ring designs symbolize your commitment to each other and your heritage.

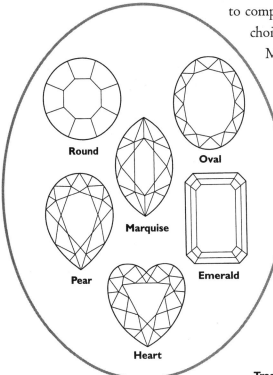

Round

Oval

Marquise

Pear

Emerald

Heart

Traditional jewel shapes

❧ *Engagement Ring Work Sheet*

Jeweler_____

Designer_____

Address _____

Phone_____

Style #_____Stone _____Setting _____

Description_____

Special elements _____

Price $_____

Jeweler_____

Designer_____

Address _____

Phone_____

Style #_____Stone _____Setting _____

Description_____

Special elements _____

Price $_____

Jeweler _____

Designer _____

Address _____

Phone _____

Style # _____ Stone _____ Setting _____

Description _____

Special elements _____

Price $ _____

Jeweler _____

Designer _____

Address _____

Phone _____

Style # _____ Stone _____ Setting _____

Description _____

Special elements _____

Price $ _____

Jeweler_____

Designer_____

Address _____

Phone_____

Style # _____Stone _____Setting _____

Description_____

Special elements _____

Price $_____

Jeweler_____

Designer_____

Address _____

Phone_____

Style # _____Stone _____Setting _____

Description_____

Special elements _____

Price $_____

Adinkra symbols are both art and meaningful representation
of important principles of African culture.

SANKOFA:
Symbol of the wisdom in learning from the past in building for the future.

DWENINI MMEN:
Symbol of strength and humility.

FUNTUMMIREKU-DENKYEM-MIREKU: Symbol of unity in diversity and warning against internal squabbles where there is a common destiny.

FAFANTO:
Symbol of tenderness, gentleness, honesty, and fragility.

OSRAM NE NSROMMA:
Symbol of faithfulness, love, harmony, fondness, loyalty, benevolence, and the feminine essence of life.

ASASE YE DURU:
Symbol of providence and the divinity of Mother Earth.

AKOMA:
Symbol of love, patience, good-will, faithfulness, and endurance.

ODO NYERA FIE KWAN:
Symbol of love, devotion, and faithfulness.

AKOMA NTOASO:
Symbol of togetherness and unity
in thought and in deed.

EBAN:
Symbol of safety, security,
and love.

NKONSONKONSON:
Symbol of unity, interdependence,
brotherhood, and cooperation.

NYAME BIRIBI WO SORO:
Symbol of hope and aspiration.

GYE NYAME:
Symbol of the omnipotence
of God.

SUNSUM:
Symbol of spiritual purity and
sanctity of the soul.

HWEHWEMUDUA:
Symbol of excellence, perfection,
knowledge, and superior quality.

KRAPA or MUSUYIDE:
Symbol of good luck, sanctity,
good spirit, and spiritual strength.

BESE SAKA:
Symbol of affluence, power, abun-
dance, togetherness, and unity.

AYA:
Symbol of endurance, defiance against
difficulties, hardiness, perserverance,
independence, and resourcefulness.

NYAME NTI:
Symbol of faith and trust in God.

NYAME DUA:
Symbol of the presence of God
and God's protection.

❧ *Purchasing Checklist*

Jeweler _____

Designer _____

Address _____

Phone _____

Style # _____ Stone _____ Setting _____

Description _____

Special elements _____

Total cost _____

Date and amount of deposit _____ /$ _____

Date and amount of final payment _____ /$ _____

INSURANCE

Once you've purchased your ring, two things are a must: first get it appraised (your jeweler will usually provide this) and then insure it. Check with your insurance broker if you have homeowner's or apartment insurance or with a local insurance company to inquire about the best plan available to you.

TAKING CARE OF BUSINESS

As you begin to announce your engagement, think carefully about your options for keeping, combining, or changing your name, not only in your social arena, but in your business and financial dealings. Use this work sheet to manage all the record keeping.

CHANGING YOUR NAME AND ADDRESS

To use checklist on the followng pages, fill in the names, addresses, and phone numbers of the companies and organizations you will need to notify. Check them off when you make your first contact and again when you follow up.

❧ *Checklist for Changing Your Name and Address*

ITEM TO CHANGE	ADDRESS

Legal Documents

Social Security _____   _____

Passport _____   _____

Voter registration _____   _____

Driver's license _____   _____

Car registration _____   _____

Insurance _____   _____

Banks

_____   _____

_____   _____

_____   _____

Credit Cards

_____   _____

_____   _____

_____   _____

Doctors

_____   _____

_____   _____

_____   _____

Utility Companies

Phone _____   _____

Gas _____   _____

Electric _____   _____

Magazine and Newspaper Subscriptions

_____   _____

_____   _____

_____   _____

Organizations and Clubs

_____   _____

_____   _____

TELEPHONE #	ACTION NEEDED	DATE HANDLED
_____	_____	_____
_____	_____	_____
_____	_____	_____
_____	_____	_____
_____	_____	_____
_____	_____	_____
_____	_____	_____
_____	_____	_____
_____	_____	_____
_____	_____	_____
_____	_____	_____
_____	_____	_____
_____	_____	_____
_____	_____	_____
_____	_____	_____
_____	_____	_____
_____	_____	_____
_____	_____	_____
_____	_____	_____
_____	_____	_____

Prenuptial agreements are usually written to protect previous arrangements one or both marriage partners have made. You may want to make sure inherited property passes to your children or other blood relatives. Sometimes parties want to safeguard previously acquired assets. Such agreements can be sensitive issues. Talk openly and do not attempt to finalize the agreement yourselves. Hire a good lawyer. (The National Bar Association, an esteemed association of African-American attorneys, can refer you to good counsel.)

❧ *Prenuptial Agreement Work Sheet*

Lawyer _____

Address _____

Phone _____

Terms _____

_____

_____

_____

_____

_____

_____

Date Signed _____

Even though prenuptial agreements are now becoming fashionable, most couples still aren't taking advantage of them. If you opt not to sign a prenuptial, it is wise to come to an understanding about what each party is bringing to the marriage. Take time now, in your own way, to discuss your assets, savings, even debts, and other material issues. We've come a long way as a people from the days when our bodies were considered property and we could not even in marriage legally give ourselves to one another. Take pride, as you begin your engagement, that you are marrying your bodies, souls, *and* fortunes together for the good of the entire African-American community.

When you plan your work and work your plan, it's all fun!

Three

PLAN YOUR PLAN:

GETTING ORGANIZED

OU HAVE A JOINT VISION and you've told everyone, so now you're ready to outline a preliminary wedding plan. This section will help you create a list of all aspects of the wedding that you know you need to accomplish, beginning with the key item, your budget.

You and your fiancé will be able to present your vision to your families and friends most effectively if you have come to an agreement between yourselves about five main issues:

Budget

❧

Timing

❧

Location

❧

Style of ceremony

❧

Size of wedding and reception

❧

You've covered the last four issues in creating your joint vision statement, so now let's tackle the item that will have the most important influence on making your vision a reality. Remember, you can achieve your goal, regardless of your budget. If you envision a large wedding with a cast of hundreds of family and friends, you can have it. Your budget will simply determine whether it is a catered event in an elegant country club or one where your family cooks all the favorite dishes as a major spread on picnic tables on the rolling lawns of your church. Your budget will define your vision, but don't let money matters deter or determine it.

BUDGET

Start by having a good discussion on nuptial budgetary matters, just the two of you. Keep in mind the creative ways African-Americans, drawing from African traditions, have financed other important celebrations—from baby dedications, to graduations, to golden anniversaries. Everyone involved usually pitches in, if not with a financial contribution then with time and labor. Let the Kwanzaa principle of *ujamaa*—cooperative economics—be your inspiration and guide. Remember that the custom of the bride's family paying for everything is *not* the custom in the Black community. The basic sources for financing are:

- ❧ You and your fiancé
- ❧ Your family and/or his family
- ❧ A cooperative plan including all of you

Money can be the most sensitive part of planning a wedding. That's why it's especially important for the two of you to first decide on a practical and acceptable form of financing. Be realistic about your own resources and those of your families. It is *not* wise to seek prices first and then build your budget around them. Assess your resources first and then plan your wedding accordingly. Use the form below to gather information on who can contribute what, and to total those contributions into the budget amount you will use in your planning. Then use the column at the right to keep track of financial resources as they are contributed. A more detailed form for individual contributors follows.

❧ *Financing Work Sheet*

	SUGGESTED	ACTUAL
Bride's family	$	$
Bride	$	$
Groom's family	$	$
Groom	$	$
Other_____	$	$
Other_____	$	$
Other_____	$	$
Other_____	$	$
Total	$	$

❧ Budget Contributor Work Sheets

Contributor _____

Amount received $ _____

Date received _____

Money applied to _____

Contributor _____

Amount received $ _____

Date received _____

Money applied to _____

Contributor _____

Amount received $ _____

Date received _____

Money applied to _____

Who Traditionally Pays for What

The Bride

- Groom's wedding ring
- Groom's wedding gift
- The services of a bridal consultant (may be shared with other contributors)
- Gifts for her attendants and other key participants
- Personal stationery
- Blood test/physical examination
- May host a pre-wedding bridesmaids' party if the bridesmaids don't
- Hair stylist and makeup artist
- Wedding gift log
- May provide housing for out-of-town guests
- Wedding guest book

The Bride's Family

- Engagement party
- Wedding gift for the bride and groom
- Bride's gown, veil, accessories, and trousseau
- Invitations, announcements, calligraphy, and postage
- Ceremony, including rental of sanctuary if necessary, fees for organist, choir, other musicians, and sexton, aisle carpets, and other decorations
- Reception, including food, beverages, music, and decorations

- Flowers, including bouquets for the bride and bridesmaids, flowers for the flower girls, boutonniere for the father of the bride, and arrangements at the ceremony and reception site
- Engagement and wedding photography/videography
- Gratuities
- Transportation for the bridal party to the ceremony and from the ceremony to the reception
- Security arrangements for the gifts

The Bridesmaids

- Bridesmaid attire
- Travel expenses
- Lodging
- Group wedding gift for the couple
- May host a shower for the bride
- May host a pre-wedding bridesmaids' party

The Bridegroom

- Bride's engagement and wedding rings
- Bride's wedding gift
- Groom's attire
- Gifts for the groomsmen
- Personal stationery
- May host bachelor party if his attendants don't
- Blood test/physical examination
- Marriage license

- Clergy fee
- Corsages for the mothers, grandmothers, and other honored female guests
- Boutonnieres for his attendants and himself
- May provide housing for out-of-town attendants

The Bridegroom's Family

- Their wedding attire, travel, and accommodations
- Wedding gift for the bride and groom
- May host a bachelor dinner
- Rehearsal dinner

The Best Man and Ushers

- Attire for the ceremony
- Travel expenses
- Lodging
- Group wedding gift
- May host the bachelor party
- Decorations for the get-away car

Out-of-Town Guests

- Travel expenses
- Lodging

Here is an example of a personally designed budget developed for a couple who married in New York City. The Budget Master column is compiled by a software program used by the couple's bridal consultant and is based on the couple's stated budget of $18,000. The Budget column shows the adjustments the couple made to the standardized budget allocations. As they used the budget sheet, they filled in the Actual Costs and Balance Due columns to keep track of expenses and expenditures. The sheet indicates the reality of most weddings—couples spend more than they plan to!

CATEGORY	BUDGET MASTER	BUDGET	ACTUAL COST	BALANCE DUE	AMOUNT OVER/UNDER
Accessories	$90.00	$106.17	$151.63	$0.00	$45.46
Bridal consultant	$2,700.00	$1,500.00	$2,632.13	$0.00	$1,132.13
Bride's attire	$900.00	$983.45	1,176.97	$0.00	$193.52
Cakes	$450.00	$350.00	$400.00	$0.00	$50.00
Ceremony	$216.00	$935.00	$1,190.00	$0.00	$255.00
Drummers	$0.00	$250.00	$275.00	$0.00	$25.00
Entertainment	$720.00	$1,300.00	$1,600.00	$0.00	$300.00
Flowers	$720.00	$433.00	$521.00	$0.00	$88.00
Gifts	$90.00	$100.00	$216.50	$0.00	$116.50
Groom's attire	$0.00	$123.99	$123.99	$0.00	$0.00
Honeymoon	$2,034.00	$2,100.00	$2,500.00	$0.00	$400.00
Invitations	$360.00	$546.66	$665.95	$0.00	$119.29
Photography	$450.00	$250.00	$400.00	$0.00	$150.00
Reception	$5,760.00	$5,150.00	$7,829.85	$0.00	$2,679.85
Rehearsal dinner	$1,080.00	$295.00	$295.00	$0.00	$0.00
Rings	$1,800.00	$2,273.25	$2,381.50	$0.00	$108.25
Transportation	$180.00	$350.00	$550.00	$0.00	$200.00
Videography	$450.00	$350.00	$600.00	$0.0	$250.00
Wedding programs	$0.00	$150.00	$185.00	$0.00	$35.00
Grand totals:	**$18,000.00**	**$17,546.52**	**$23,694.52**	**$0.00**	**$6,148.00**

Pay careful attention to the budget items, and decide which are important to you. Perhaps you will spend a lot on rings and have no videography at all. Now is where your joint vision really comes into play. You will not finalize your budget until you have made decisions about your ceremony and reception, however you can now make a working draft. Refer to the Master Budget Work Sheet below. It is repeated here with lots of space for you to customize it for your own use.

∾ *Master Budget*

CATEGORY	BUDGET	ACTUAL COST	BALANCE DUE	AMOUNT OVER/UNDER
Accessories	_____	_____	_____	_____
Balloon decorations	_____	_____	_____	_____
Bridal consultant	_____	_____	_____	_____
Bride's attire	_____	_____	_____	_____
Cakes	_____	_____	_____	_____
Ceremony	_____	_____	_____	_____
Drummers	_____	_____	_____	_____
Entertainment	_____	_____	_____	_____
Flowers	_____	_____	_____	_____

Category	Budget	Actual Cost	Balance Due	Amount Over/Under
Gifts	_____	_____	_____	_____
Groom's attire	_____	_____	_____	_____
Honeymoon	_____	_____	_____	_____
Invitations	_____	_____	_____	_____
Photography	_____	_____	_____	_____
Reception	_____	_____	_____	_____
Rehearsal dinner	_____	_____	_____	_____
Rings	_____	_____	_____	_____
Transportation	_____	_____	_____	_____
Videography	_____	_____	_____	_____
Wedding programs	_____	_____	_____	_____
Grand totals:	_____	_____	_____	_____

Now think about each item in the Master Budget Work Sheet, and check off each service you feel you will require for your wedding, projecting an amount you can afford to spend for that item. Your projected budget total should be comparable to your actual budget amount. Every single item you have just projected will change, however, this initial projection will be your budgetary guide as you price goods and services for your wedding, juggling and prioritizing as you do. Now you're ready to shop for vendors. As you begin to shop, carefully think about all the available alternatives in relation to your budget, because the financing will influence every aspect of your wedding and set the tone for how your marital financial life begins.

DIVIDE THE WORK

Before you begin to shop for vendors for the myriad items and services you'll need for your wedding, take a moment to evaluate the time involved and your schedules. If you're like most couples, the Master Budget Work Sheet made you sweat, not only because you first realized the financial scope of this celebration but because it also gave you a glimpse of the many facets of the planning.

Consider now whether you'll do all the planning yourselves or hire a wedding consultant or assemble a team of family and friends to help. Remember, as you get deeper into your wedding plans and closer to your Big Day, the pre-wedding festivities that everyone has planned for you may prevent you from attending to the last-minute details. You'll need to ask relatives and friends to help you with them. So it's best to create a work plan now. Identify what you need to accomplish and who you feel will be capable of handling it for you. Use the following work sheets to help you get started.

❧ *Wedding Tasks List*

HELPER

1. _____
2. _____
3. _____
4. _____
5. _____
6. _____
7. _____
8. _____
9. _____
10. _____
11. _____
12. _____
13. _____
14. _____
15. _____

PHONE   **SKILL/AREA**

_____   _____

_____   _____

_____   _____

_____   _____

_____   _____

_____   _____

_____   _____

_____   _____

_____   _____

_____   _____

_____   _____

_____   _____

❧ *Task Assignments List*

Task _____

Assigned to _____

Date due _____

Task _____

Assigned to _____

Date due _____

Task _____

Assigned to _____

Date due _____

Task _____

Assigned to _____

Date due _____

Task _____

Assigned to _____

Date due _____

While we've designed this book to be your very own wedding consultant, no book can approach what a real live person can accomplish. We recommend using a professional wedding consultant if at all possible, especially if time is short, you both have demands on your time, or if your wedding will be large, complex, or not in the same city as where you live. Kinds of consultants and fee options range from full service to wedding day only, from flat fees to hourly rates, so you should be able to find professional help to suit your needs and budget. Here's a work sheet to get you started:

❧ *Wedding Consultant Work Sheet*

Estimate #1

Company name _____

Consultant/planner's name _____

Address _____

_____

Phone_____Fax_____

Appointment date _____Time_____

Services to be rendered _____

_____

Consultant's fee $ _____

   ❑ Percentage ❑ Hourly ❑ Flat fee *(check one)*

Amount of deposit $ _____ Date of deposit _____

2nd payment amount $ _____ Date due _____

Final payment $ _____ Date due _____

Date contract signed _____

References _____

Comment _____

Estimate #2

Company name _____

Consultant/planner's name _____

Address _____

_____

Phone _____ Fax _____

Appointment date _____ Time _____

Services to be rendered _____

_____

Consultant's fee $ _____

    ❏ Percentage   ❏ Hourly   ❏ Flat fee *(check one)*

Amount of deposit $ _____ Date of deposit _____

2nd payment amount $ _____ Date due _____

Final payment $ _____ Date due _____

Date contract signed _____

References _____

Comment _____

Estimate #3

Company name _____

Consultant/planner's name _____

Address _____

_____

Phone_____Fax_____

Appointment date _____Time_____

Services to be rendered _____

_____

Consultant's fee $ _____

    ❏ Percentage ❏ Hourly ❏ Flat fee *(check one)*

Amount of deposit $ _____ Date of deposit _____

2nd payment amount $ _____ Date due _____

Final payment $ _____ Date due _____

Date contract signed_____

References _____

Comment _____

    Be sure to get a contract from your bridal consultant that lists her exact duties and services and costs.

    For a bridal consultant in your area, contact the Association of Bridal Consultants by telephoning 860-355-0464.

The contract with your bridal consultant will be the first of several contracts you will sign in the process of planning your wedding. It is imperative that you get signed contracts/agreements from your service providers, which will spell out exactly what you're getting for your money. After you have selected the vendors, keep copies of the contracts. Periodically, review them to make sure the services or delivery dates are being met according to contract and that you have not forgotten a second or final payment date. A good way to keep track is to set up a scheduler on your computer. This is a good way to keep track of the budget, as well.

If a vendor does not provide a written proposal and contract, we suggest that you think twice before making an agreement. Proposals and contracts protect you *and* the vendor.

If you and your fiancé still want to employ the services of a provider that does not have a contract then you need to draw one up. Make certain that the proprietor or manager of the business signs it. The business should get one copy, and you retain a copy for your files. *Hint: it is a good idea to bring every contract you sign with you on your wedding day. Ask your bridal consultant or a family member to hold them for you. This way, you have them should you need to refer to them.*

A contract tells a story. It should specify everything you are ordering and everything the vendor is to provide. Of course, general information such as date and location of wedding, set-up time, quantity ordered, contact person on-site, and cost and payment structure must be included.

But there is more than just the general information that needs to be included. You need details: color, size, how something is to be arranged. For example, a contract with your florist should include not only color and bouquet style, but what flowers you are ordering; how many of each flower is to be included in a centerpiece and a bouquet; what accessories, if any, are to be included and how they are to be incorporated. If the florist is providing glass mirrors as part of the centerpiece, who owns them? If a candle is to be lit on the tables, who is responsible for the lighting? Ask the florist to sketch on the contract how the centerpieces and/or bouquets will be arranged, based on your agreement.

When dealing with a balloon artist, you need to know not only the colors of the balloons to be used, but the sizes. Will they be air-filled or helium-filled? Are they to be high-floated and what type of ribbons are to be used? Is the decorator to provide a guest book, wishing well, or other accessories? Where are they to be placed?

The intricate details may not seem important at first, but they become so the day of the wedding. If you ordered glitter to be lightly dusted on your tables and find when you enter your reception party that it is not there, your vendor may or may not be responsible. If it's not on the contract, they are not responsible. But if it is clearly on the contract, then it is their problem to correct.

Ask the vendor how changes to the contract are handled. "We have an agreed understanding with our clients that if any changes need to be made the day of the wedding, because of room constraints, etc., we have permission to do so," says Arlene Kronowitz, president of A Whimsical Expression.

Should you and your groom change your mind on something that will require the contract to be altered, call your vendor as soon as possible. The present contract should be null and void and a revised contract drawn up. Kronowitz suggests that the contract clearly state that the contract is revised and that both parties initial it.

Most vendors will not allow major changes to be made two weeks prior to the event. But should minor changes be made, whether by you or your vendor, they should be discussed first, then added to the contract and initialed by both parties.

READY, SET, PLAN

You already made your key decisions regarding timing, location, style of ceremony, and site of the wedding and reception when you recorded your joint vision. The following forms will allow you to put the details down on paper where you can readily refer to them as you plan.

Timing. Timing (date and time of day) is everything. Be sure that when recording your joint vision, you took into account any factors that may affect the date of your wedding: school calendars, job transfers, the availability of your nearest and dearest. The time of year and the time of day you choose can also affect the cost of your wedding: ceremonies during the prime marrying months of May to October and evening weddings are generally more expensive, and the most popular sites are often booked several years in advance. In order to secure the location of your dreams, allow enough planning—at least twelve to fourteen months—and decide on one or two backup dates in case your site of choice is not available. It's a possibility that your first date may not work for various reasons: that choice location that you envision for your chosen date might be booked, those dear to you might not be able to attend on your planned date, or other service providers you feel are essential to creating your special day might have conflicts.

Record below your first choice of the month, day, and year in which you would like to marry (from your joint vision), then decide on your second and third choices.

	MONTH	DAY	YEAR
First choice	_____	_____	_____
Second choice	_____	_____	_____
Third choice	_____	_____	_____

Location: You have already noted this in your joint vision on page 9. If where you want to hold your ceremony is connected to when you have it and who will be able to officiate or attend, be sure to keep the location in mind if the when and who changes.

Style of Ceremony. The style of ceremony you noted in your joint vision will influence your financing, timing, and location. Describe in the space provided below more details of what you have in mind for a style.

Description of key style elements_____

_____

_____

_____

_____

_____

_____

_____

Possible Officiant(s) _____

_____

_____

Size. In your joint vision, you decided on the general size of your wedding, and now you need to set some specific parameters on the number of people you want to invite. Remember, your parents, attendants, and yourselves are included in the number that you will use in picking the ceremony and reception sites and give to the caterer.

The smallest wedding has honor attendants (maid/matron of honor and best man) to stand as witnesses. These may be a sister, brother, and in some cases, father of the bridegroom as best man and mother of the bride as matron of honor. You may also want to include close family members and friends as bridesmaids; groomsmen; ushers; junior bridesmaids, groomsmen, and ushers; flower girls; ring bearers; train bearers; hosts and hostesses. Before inviting them to participate, be considerate, keeping in mind the costs involved in buying their own wedding outfits and perhaps long-distance travel and hotel expenses. You must also consider what costs *you* will incur to have them participate. Will the cost of additional bouquets and gifts stretch your budget? Will there be enough space at the altar area to hold more than two attendants?

The Wedding Party:
A Description of Each Role

Your Queen Diva (Maid or Matron of Honor)

- Helps coordinate bridesmaids' activities before and during ceremony
- Attends all pre-wedding parties
- May arrange bridal shower
- May help record shower and wedding gifts
- May act as an official witness for the marriage license
- Unofficially calms the bride's nerves
- Helps bride dress for the ceremony and for departure from the reception
- Greets the officiant(s) if the wedding is at home
- Arranges wedding gown train before the processional and rearranges for the recessional (if there are no pages)
- Holds bride's bouquet and gloves during the ceremony, and the groom's wedding ring
- Bustles the bride's train and removes headpiece before the reception
- Keeps track of bride's personal items at ceremony and reception
- Stands next to the couple in the receiving line
- Helps with introductions of guests and with directing photographer at reception
- Sits on the bridegroom's left at the bridal table

Your Princess Divas (Bridesmaids)

- Help with pre-wedding activities and errands
- Attend all pre-wedding parties
- May co-host bridesmaids' lunch or bachelorette party

- May help to prepare wedding favors and place cards
- Stand with the couple in the receiving line
- Circulate at the reception, acting as deputy hostesses

Little Divas (Junior Bridesmaids)

- Usually 10–14 years old
- Walk with the bridal party
- May be dressed in smaller versions of the bridesmaids' dresses or in dresses more appropriate for their ages
- May stand in the receiving line

Your Man's Main Man (Best Man)

- Attends all pre-wedding parties the bridegroom attends
- May act as second official witness for the marriage license
- Makes sure groom arrives on time, properly dressed and prepared!
- Does not walk in the processional
- Oversees the ushers; designates those who will escort the immediate family
- Keeps rings, license, and any honeymoon tickets safely tucked away
- Holds the bride's wedding ring during the ceremony
- Delivers the officiant's fee
- Stands in the receiving line
- Keeps track of the bridegroom's personal items at the reception
- Delivers the first toast at reception
- Helps the bridegroom change for the honeymoon getaway
- Makes sure all the luggage for the bride and groom is put into the getaway car

Buffalo Soldiers (Groomsmen/Ushers)

- Assist the groom with any pre-wedding, wedding, and post-wedding duties
- Attend the pre-wedding parties the groom attends
- Seat guests at ceremony
- Unroll the aisle runner after the bride's mother is seated
- Decorate the getaway car

Little Buffalo Soldiers (Junior Ushers)

- Usually 10–14 years old
- Don't usher guests but may put the pew ribbons in place
- Walk in the processional and recessional

Pint-sized Petal Pusher (Flower Girl)

- Usually 5–7 years old
- Immediately precedes the bride in the processional, tossing petals along the runner
- May carry guestbook around at the reception to collect signatures

Rubber Band Mini-Man (Ring Bearer)

- Carries clever substitutes for the wedding bands to the altar tied with ribbons to a satin pillow
- Walks right before the flower girl in the processional; beside her in the recessional

Pages

- Walk with the bridal party in the processional and recessional

Train Bearers

- Walk in a pair right behind the bride and carry her train up and down the aisle

Wedding Party Work Sheet

NAME

Honor attendants

Tiphanie Todd
Natasha Pittman

Bridesmaids

Taesha Spencer
Lisa Saunders
Jaki

Junior bridesmaids

Javita Person

Best man

Chip

Groomsmen

Head usher

_____

_____

_____

Ushers

_____

_____

_____

Junior ushers

_____

_____

Ring bearer

Carlton Smith

_____

_____

Train bearers

_____

_____

_____

Page

_____

_____

_____

❧ *Wedding Party Contact Work Sheet*

NAME OF ATTENDANT	PHONE

ADDRESS   **CITY/STATE/ZIP**

_____   _____

_____   _____

_____   _____

_____   _____

_____   _____

_____   _____

_____   _____

_____   _____

_____   _____

_____   _____

_____   _____

Making the guest list lets everyone enjoy the anticipation of gathering friends and family together for the happy occasion. Photocopy the work sheets below to make sure everyone has enough sheets. Keep all the lists, as you will undoubtedly expand or contract your master list, and these lists will help you in this process.

❧ Bride's Guest List

Name(s)_____   Name(s)_____

Address _____   Address _____

City/state/zip _____   City/state/zip _____

Phone _____   Phone _____

Name(s)_____   Name(s)_____

Address _____   Address _____

City/state/zip _____   City/state/zip _____

Phone _____   Phone _____

Name(s)_____   Name(s)_____

Address _____   Address _____

City/state/zip _____   City/state/zip _____

Phone _____   Phone _____

Name(s)_____   Name(s)_____

Address _____   Address _____

City/state/zip _____   City/state/zip _____

Phone_____   Phone_____

Name(s)_____   Name(s)_____

Address _____   Address _____

City/state/zip _____   City/state/zip _____

Phone_____   Phone_____

Name(s)_____   Name(s)_____

Address _____   Address _____

City/state/zip _____   City/state/zip _____

Phone_____   Phone_____

Name(s)_____   Name(s)_____

Address _____   Address _____

City/state/zip _____   City/state/zip _____

Phone_____   Phone_____

🖎 *Bridegroom's Guest List*

Name(s)_____   Name(s)_____

Address _____   Address _____

City/state/zip _____   City/state/zip _____

Phone _____   Phone _____

Name(s)_____   Name(s)_____

Address _____   Address _____

City/state/zip _____   City/state/zip _____

Phone _____   Phone _____

Name(s)_____   Name(s)_____

Address _____   Address _____

City/state/zip _____   City/state/zip _____

Phone _____   Phone _____

Name(s)_____   Name(s)_____

Address _____   Address _____

City/state/zip _____   City/state/zip _____

Phone _____   Phone _____

❧ *Bride's Parents' Guest List*

Name(s)_____   Name(s)_____

Address _____   Address _____

City/state/zip _____   City/state/zip _____

Phone_____   Phone_____

Name(s)_____   Name(s)_____

Address _____   Address _____

City/state/zip _____   City/state/zip _____

Phone_____   Phone_____

Name(s)_____   Name(s)_____

Address _____   Address _____

City/state/zip _____   City/state/zip _____

Phone_____   Phone_____

Name(s)_____   Name(s)_____

Address _____   Address _____

City/state/zip _____   City/state/zip _____

Phone_____   Phone_____

❧ *Bridegroom's Parents' Guest List*

Name(s)_____   Name(s)_____

Address _____   Address _____

City/state/zip _____   City/state/zip _____

Phone _____   Phone _____

Name(s)_____   Name(s)_____

Address _____   Address _____

City/state/zip _____   City/state/zip _____

Phone _____   Phone _____

Name(s)_____   Name(s)_____

Address _____   Address _____

City/state/zip _____   City/state/zip _____

Phone _____   Phone _____

Name(s)_____   Name(s)_____

Address _____   Address _____

City/state/zip _____   City/state/zip _____

Phone _____   Phone _____

❧ *Master Guest List*

Name(s) _____

Address _____

City/state/zip _____

Phone _____

Number in party _____

Date invitation sent _____

Total acceptances _____   Total regrets _____

Gift _____   Date received _____   Thank You sent _____

Name(s) _____

Address _____

City/state/zip _____

Phone _____

Number in party _____

Date invitation sent _____

Total acceptances _____   Total regrets _____

Gift _____   Date received _____   Thank You sent _____

Name(s) _____

Address _____

City/state/zip _____

Phone _____

Number in party _____

Date invitation sent _____

Total acceptances _____ Total regrets _____

Gift _____ Date received _____ Thank You sent _____

Name(s) _____

Address _____

City/state/zip _____

Phone _____

Number in party _____

Date invitation sent _____

Total acceptances _____ Total regrets _____

Gift _____ Date received _____ Thank You sent _____

Name(s) _____

Address _____

City/state/zip _____

Phone _____

Number in party _____

Date invitation sent _____

Total acceptances _____   Total regrets _____

Gift _____   Date received _____   Thank You sent _____

Name(s) _____

Address _____

City/state/zip _____

Phone _____

Number in party _____

Date invitation sent _____

Total acceptances _____   Total regrets _____

Gift _____   Date received _____   Thank You sent _____

❧ *Total Guest List*

INVITED BY	NUMBER
Bride _____	_____
Groom_____	_____
Bride's parents_____	_____
Groom's parents _____	_____
Other _____	_____
Other _____	_____
Other _____	_____
Other _____	_____
Total_____	_____

The number of guests you decide upon will affect the other elements of your plan. Keeping the guest list small may allow you to have a seated dinner or travel to a faraway location. On the other hand, perhaps having all your friends and relatives attend is more important to you than food or location. Rest assured that you can accomplish all of the above with careful, practical planning.

Look back on your work. You now have a written vision of your wedding with specific, practical details that you both agree upon. You have an idea of all the essential elements and suggestions on who will contribute the money that will comprise your total budget. Think of this as your draft vision. It will change as you proceed with the planning, but look back on it now and circle the elements you feel are essential to your happiness. It's those elements that you will not want to compromise in the give and take that the day-to-day planning will inevitably require. Plan in hand, let's begin the legwork.

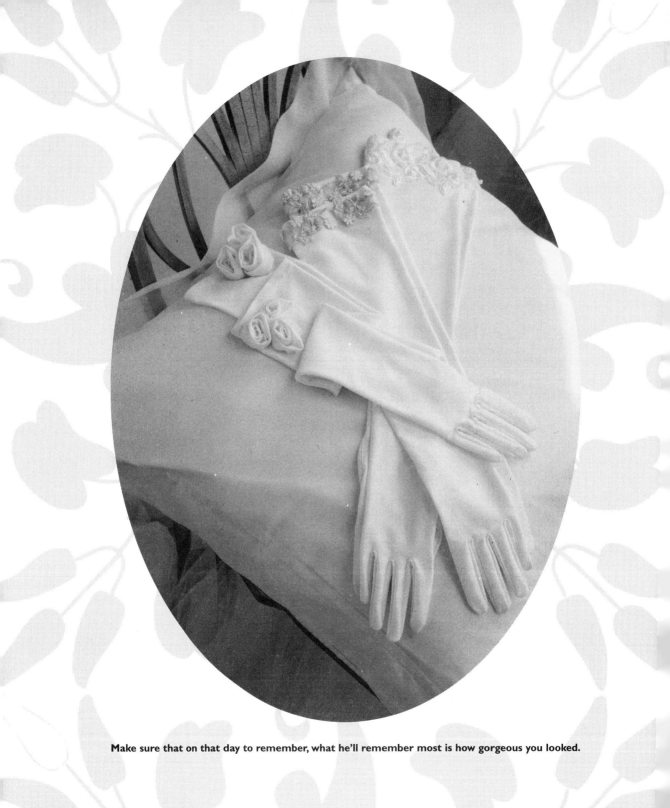

Make sure that on that day to remember, what he'll remember most is how gorgeous you looked.

Four

YOUR SIGNATURE FASHION

BRIDE'S ATTIRE

K, WE ADMIT IT. You're supposed to book the reception

hall and lock in a date at the church or wherever you're having the ceremony. Finding the

place is the most important thing in planning a wedding, say the experts, whoever they

are. And while we at *Signature Bride* agree with the experts and advise you to plan proper-

ly and well, we say *you* are the most important thing in your wedding plans. Whether you

African Wedding Attire

The peoples and cultures of Africa are many and varied—from traditional ethnic groups such as the Yoruba of Nigeria to Christians and Muslims, each with their own wedding customs and style of dress.

The Yoruba People of Southern Nigeria.

Aso oke is a hand-woven fabric of cotton and silk with metallic (silver and/or gold) threads customarily worn by the Yoruba people at weddings. The bride would have to request this fabric in her choice of color three to six months before her ceremony.

Traditional Yoruba attire for the bride is a four-piece wrap set, including a *boubah* (blouse), *iro* (wrap skirt), *iborun* (shawl), and a *gele* (head wrap).

The bridegroom would wear a four-piece garment consisting of an *agabada* (a long ceremonial robe) worn over a *dashiki* (a tunic top and long pants) with a *fila* (hat).

The Christian Nigerian.

Christian Nigerians celebrate weddings for three days. On the first day, a Friday, the couple must get permission from their families and the blessing of their elders to marry. On Saturday, the ceremony takes place, with the bride wearing either a wrap of *aso oke* or a European-style wedding gown. Sunday is then the Day of Thanksgiving, when the new bride wears a dress of white or off-white lace or a combination of *aso oke* and lace.

Muslim.

Fatou Ndeye Sall, a Manhattan-based designer of African-style garments, tells us that in Muslim parts of Africa, the bride wears three different outfits in one day of celebration. She walks to a nearby "beauty place" (parlor) for each change of clothing and also refreshens her makeup.

From 10 A.M. to 1 P.M., she wears a *taille basse*, a European-style form-fitting dress. From 1 P.M. to 5 P.M., she wears a *mamboye*, an African loose-fitting outfit with a wrapped skirt and head wrap. From 5 P.M. to 9 P.M., she dons a Western-style white bridal dress.

get married in a tent or a tree house, *you* are the star attraction. So skip ahead to the next chapter if you think a few days of shopping will make you miss out on the reception and ceremony sites of your dreams. But we advise you to concentrate for the first few days of your planning on *looking* like a dream.

Grab a strapless bra and your best shopping partner and start looking at dresses. If there's a special item you're determined to wear when you say the big "I do" take it along, and bring shoes that make you just the height you plan to be beside your brand-new husband. If you are a shop-till-you-drop sister, planning a wedding will be the most fun you can have with your clothes off (well, almost).

Before you rev up the engine and head for the mall or flag a cab to the stores downtown, double back to your joint wedding vision. The wedding style you chose will help you define your shopping hemisphere. If you're going to be a storybook princess bride, you'll look in different shops than if you picture yourself an African bride-queen.

Your options are many, from custom-made, off the rack, to specially designed gowns. Regardless of your final choice, we recommend at least a leisurely afternoon of looking at a wide variety of dresses before you buy, order, or commission that once-in-a-lifetime attire.

Photocopy the work sheets in this chapter as often as you need to. And, yes, write in all of the picky details. You'll be glad you did as you comparison shop, and you'll be superglad you did when you're trying to recall the fabric of your wedding gown on your fiftieth anniversary.

Copy the pages for the men, too, and the entire wedding party will rib you for being a general but will secretly be grateful if you copy pages for them to record their information. Wedding shopping is serious business, and trying to recall from memory all the choices can take some of the fun out of the whole process. You know how you

Afrocentric wedding attire—high style and heritage begin your happily ever aftering.

feel after a shop-till-you-drop day at the mall. Multiply that times a zillion, and that's what it's like shopping for wedding attire without a record keeper.

The Traditional Wedding Gown

Silhouettes

BALLGOWN: fitted waist and bodice with a full skirt

BASQUE: similar to the ballgown, but waist drops to a point in the front

EMPIRE: high-waisted (below the bust) with a narrower skirt

MERMAID: hugs the body to the knees, where the skirt flares out

PRINCESS: closely fitted from shoulder to waist (which has no seam) with a skirt that then tapers out to the floor

SHEATH: follows the contour of the body from the shoulder down

Necklines

BERTHA: high neck with a capelike collar that covers the shoulders

FICHU: low-cut, with an attached scarflike garment piece that drapes around neckline

JEWEL: just around the base of the throat

QUEEN ANNE: rises to the base of the neck in the back, frames the shoulders and scoops low in the front

SABRINA: from the tip of one shoulder to the other, in front and back

SWEETHEART: shaped like the top of a heart

Sleeves

BALLOON: full, gathered, elbow-length

CAP: just caps the shoulder

DOLMAN: sleeve cut in one piece with the bodice, wide at the shoulder (with no shoulder seam), and often narrowing to the wrist

FITTED POINT: long, slim sleeve that ends in a point just below the wrist

GAUNTLET: removable sleeve that extends from just above the elbow to the wrist

LEG OF MUTTON: full from the shoulder to the elbow, then fitted to the wrist

PAGODA: fitted from the shoulder to the elbow, then flares out in tiered layers to the mid-arm in front and the wrist in back

Trains

SWEEP: extends 8–12 inches on the floor

CHAPEL: extends 3½–4½ feet from the waist

CATHEDRAL: extends 6½–7½ feet from the waist

EXTENDED CATHEDRAL: extends 12 feet or more from the waist

Fabrics

CHARMEUSE: a liquid, slinky fabric, usually silk

CHIFFON: soft, sheer, lightweight fabric of cotton, silk, nylon, or rayon

CREPE: soft, crinkled fabric

DEVORE: a patterned velvet in which some of the pile has been removed to expose the underlying weave; gives the appearance of a kind of velvet lace

ORGANZA: sheer and lightweight as chiffon, but with a stiff finish

PANNE: a shiny, slinky velvet

SATIN: a kind of weave that adds sheen to the surface of a fabric, usually cotton or silk

SHANTUNG: a heavier silk with a nubby texture

TAFFETA: a lightweight, crisp, shiny silk

TULLE: a fine net, usually of silk or nylon, often used for veils or overskirts

Gorgeous wedding style is for women of all sizes.

❧ *Bridal Gown Work Sheet*

Retail shop _____ Sales rep _____

Address _____

_____ Phone _____

Designer _____ Style _____ Fabric _____

Color _____ Size _____

Budget amount $ _____ Actual cost $ _____

Retail shop _____ Sales rep _____

Address _____

_____ Phone _____

Designer _____ Style _____ Fabric _____

Color _____ Size _____

Budget amount $ _____ Actual cost $ _____

Retail shop _____ Sales rep _____

Address _____

_____ Phone _____

Designer _____ Style _____ Fabric _____

Color _____ Size _____

Budget amount $ _____ Actual cost $ _____

The seamstress will ask you to bring your wedding shoes and undergarment to a fitting for the alteration of your gown.

❧ *Wedding Gown Purchase and Fitting Work Sheet*

First Fitting

Date _____Time _____

Notes _____

Second Fitting

Date _____Time _____

Notes _____

Third Fitting

Date _____Time _____

Notes _____

Deposit date _____Amount paid $ _____

Date balance due _____Amount due $ _____

Delivery/pickup date _____

To be delivered to (address) _____

Notes _____

_____

_____

_____

_____

Gloves add a tasteful dazzle to a formal gown and an opportunity to
dazzle him as you . . . remove them.

Traditional Veils

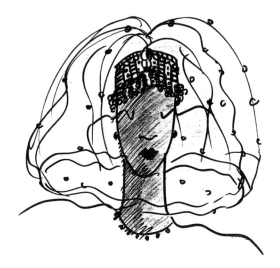

Blusher: veil that just covers the face and is turned back for the ceremonial first kiss. Sometimes attached to a longer veil.

Flyaway: multiple layers that fall to the shoulders. Worn with shorter gowns or to expose the back.

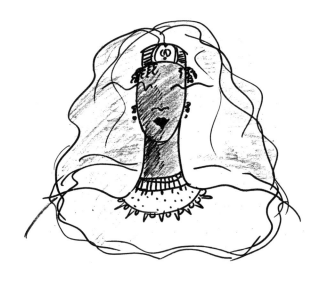

Ballerina-length: **falls to the ankles.**

Fingertip: **several layers that fall to the fingertips.**

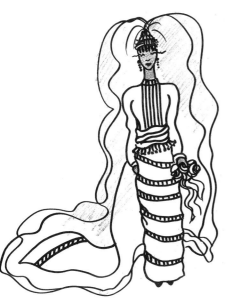

Cathedral-length: **flows three-and-a-half yards from the headpiece. Worn with a cathedral-length train.**

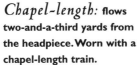

Chapel-length: **flows two-and-a-third yards from the headpiece. Worn with a chapel-length train.**

❧ *Accessories List*

	RETAIL SHOP	DESIGNER
Headpiece	_____	_____
Veil	_____	_____
Shoes	_____	_____
Trousseau	_____	_____
Hosiery	_____	_____
Gloves	_____	_____
Handbag	_____	_____
Jewelry	_____	_____

STYLE/ITEM#	COLOR	FABRIC	SIZE	COST

Total cost $ _____

Black Designers of Note

Today there are many Black fashion designers for wedding wear, and their work covers a wide spectrum of styles, from Afrocentric to traditional European. Some also include mother-of-the-bride, wedding night, and honeymoon fashions in their line.

African Fashion Apparel
Sugarland, Texas
281-530-2376

Anyiam's Creations International
Thony Anyiam
Langley Park, Maryland
301-439-1110

Cassandra Bromfield Designs
Cassandra Bromfield
Brooklyn, New York
718-398-1050

Elegant Brides
Jacqui Scott
Hallandale, Florida
954-458-0229

Ferandun Fashions
June Terry
Manhattan, New York
212-698-6389

Franklin Rowe International
Franklin Rowe
Manhattan, New York
212-967-8763

Images of Royalty International, Inc.
Rev. Doris Tongo
The Bronx, New York
718-328-5484

Ites International
Millie David
Atlanta, Georgia
770-916-1142

JRH Millinery (*headwear, more suited to bridesmaids and mothers-of-the-bride*)
Johnnye Hansford
Plainfield, New Jersey
908-753-7214

Laurie's Fashions
Laurie A. Sanders
Queens, New York
718-217-2899

Mario Uomo

    Bruce Mario Gage

    Chicago, Illinois

    312-829-UOMO

Michael Joseph Designs

    Michael Joseph

    Chicago, Illinois

    708-388-7435

Nigerian Fabrics and Fashions

    Jonathan and Boyega Adewumi

    Brooklyn, New York

    1-800-ADEWUM6

Only VanEssa!

    VanEssa Holley

    Brooklyn, New York

    1-888-MY TOUCH

Phenomenal Women Design

    Cookie Washington

    Charleston, South Carolina

    843-769-4927

The Private Stock Collection (wedding night and honeymoon wear)

    Lottie Farahh

    St. Louis, Missouri

    314-426-7761

Shirley's Bridal and Pageants, Inc.

    Shirley Jenkins

    Elgin, Illinois

    847-468-0337

Suädé

    Abdur Rahman

    Newark, New Jersey

    973-639-1083

TMF Designs, Inc.

    Therez Fleetwood

    Manhattan, New York

    212-714-8058

❧ *Work Sheet for the Bride's Attendants' Attire*

Name _____ Role _____

Retail shop _____ Sales rep _____

Address _____

_____ Phone _____

Bridesmaid's dress style _____ Fabric _____

Designer _____ Color _____ Size _____

Cost $ _____

Name _____ Role _____

Retail shop _____ Sales rep _____

Address _____

_____ Phone _____

Bridesmaid's dress style _____ Fabric _____

Designer _____ Color _____ Size _____

Cost $ _____

Name _____   Role _____

Retail shop _____   Sales rep _____

Address _____

_____   Phone _____

Bridesmaid's dress style _____   Fabric _____

Designer _____   Color _____   Size _____

Cost $ _____

Name _____   Role _____

Retail shop _____   Sales rep _____

Address _____

_____   Phone _____

Bridesmaid's dress style _____   Fabric _____

Designer _____   Color _____   Size _____

Cost $ _____

🐦 *Bridesmaid's Accessories List*

	RETAIL SHOP	DESIGNER
Headpiece	_____	_____
Shoes	_____	_____
Hosiery	_____	_____
Gloves	_____	_____
Handbag	_____	_____
Jewelry	_____	_____

STYLE/ITEM#	COLOR	FABRIC	SIZE	COST

Total cost $ _____

Work Sheet for the Bride's and Groom's Mothers' Attire

Retail shop_____ Sales rep_____

Address _____

_____ Phone _____

Dress style_____ Fabric _____

Designer_____ Color_____ Size_____

Cost $ _____

Retail shop_____ Sales rep_____

Address _____

_____ Phone _____

Dress style_____ Fabric _____

Designer_____ Color_____ Size_____

Cost $ _____

Retail shop_____ Sales rep_____

Address _____

_____ Phone _____

Dress style_____ Fabric _____

Designer_____ Color_____ Size_____

Cost $ _____

Retail shop_____ Sales rep_____

Address _____

_____ Phone _____

Dress style_____ Fabric _____

Designer_____ Color_____ Size_____

Cost $ _____

❧ Bride's Mother's Accessories List

	RETAIL SHOP	DESIGNER
Headpiece	_____	_____
Shoes	_____	_____
Hosiery	_____	_____
Gloves	_____	_____
Handbag	_____	_____
Jewelry	_____	_____

STYLE/ITEM#	COLOR	FABRIC	SIZE	COST
_____	_____	_____	_____	_____
_____	_____	_____	_____	_____
_____	_____	_____	_____	_____
_____	_____	_____	_____	_____
_____	_____	_____	_____	_____
_____	_____	_____	_____	_____

Total cost $ _____

✒ Groom's Mother's Accessories List

	RETAIL SHOP	**DESIGNER**
Headpiece	_____	_____
Shoes	_____	_____
Hosiery	_____	_____
Gloves	_____	_____
Handbag	_____	_____
Jewelry	_____	_____

STYLE/ITEM#	COLOR	FABRIC	SIZE	COST
_____	_____	_____	_____	_____
_____	_____	_____	_____	_____
_____	_____	_____	_____	_____
_____	_____	_____	_____	_____
_____	_____	_____	_____	_____
_____	_____	_____	_____	_____

Total cost $ _____

Traditional Guidelines for Formal, Semi-Formal, and Informal Wedding Attire

Formal Daytime (before 6 P.M.)

BRIDE: Floor-length gown with train and coordinating veil, gloves, shoes, and hosiery

BRIDESMAIDS: Long or short dresses with coordinating gloves, shoes, and hosiery

BRIDEGROOM AND GROOMSMEN (AND FATHERS): Gray morning (cutaway) coats, gray striped trousers, gray vests and ascots or four-in-hand ties, optional top hats, spats, and gray gloves

MOTHERS: Long or short dresses, coordinating (optional) hats, gloves, shoes, and hosiery

Formal Evening (after 6 P.M.)

BRIDE: Floor-length gown with train and coordinating veil, gloves, shoes, and hosiery

BRIDESMAIDS: Long dresses with coordinating gloves, shoes, and hosiery

BRIDEGROOM AND GROOMSMEN (AND FATHERS): White tie—full dress, with black tails, white formal shirt with wing collar, white pique vest and white bow tie, optional top hats and gloves

MOTHERS: Long or short evening dresses with coordinating (optional) hats, gloves, shoes, and hosiery

Semi-Formal Daytime (before 6 P.M.)

BRIDE: Long or short gown with coordinating veil or hat, gloves, shoes, and hosiery

BRIDESMAIDS: Dresses no longer than the bride's, with coordinating (optional) gloves, shoes, and hosiery

BRIDEGROOM AND GROOMSMEN (AND FATHERS): Gray strollers with striped trousers, pearl-gray vests, white formal shirts, four-in-hand ties, and optional homburg and gray gloves

MOTHERS: Long or short dresses with coordinating (optional) gloves, shoes, and hosiery

Semi-Formal Evening (after 6 P.M.)

BRIDE: Long or short gown with coordinating veil, gloves, shoes, and hosiery

BRIDESMAIDS: Dresses no longer than the bride's with coordinating (optional) gloves, shoes, and hosiery

BRIDEGROOM AND GROOMSMEN (AND FATHERS): Black tuxedos (or white dinner jackets with tuxedo pant for summer or warm climates), white formal shirt, vest or cummerbund, bow tie

MOTHERS: Long or short dresses with coordinating (optional) gloves, shoes, and hosiery

Informal, Daytime and Evening

BRIDE: Long or short dress or suit with (optional) hat or veil, (optional) gloves, shoes, and hosiery

BRIDESMAIDS: Dresses or suits no longer than the bride's, (optional) gloves, shoes, and hosiery

BRIDEGROOM AND GROOMSMEN (AND FATHERS): Business suits or blazers with trousers of a color and weight appropriate for the season and time of day

MOTHERS: Long or short dresses or suits with (optional) gloves, shoes, and hosiery

"Heart, be still!" you'll say to yourself when you catch a glimpse of him—all betuxed—

at the altar, as you begin your last stroll as a single woman down the aisle.

t's a myth men don't like to shop. Brothers love to shop. So turn him loose with his *boyz* or make it a togetherness outing, with you sneaking back into the men's dressing room to check his fittings. Either way, don't let him shop without this work sheet.

ᕃ *Work Sheet for the Bridegroom's Attire*

Retail shop _____ Sales rep_____

Address _____

_____ Phone_____

Tuxedo style _____ Fabric _____

Afrocentric style _____ Fabric _____

Designer_____ Color _____ Size_____

Budget amount $_____ Rental amount $_____

Delivery/pickup by_____

Return by _____

Retail shop _____ Sales rep_____

Address _____

_____ Phone_____

Tuxedo style _____ Fabric _____

Afrocentric style _____ Fabric _____

Designer_____ Color _____ Size_____

Budget amount $_____ Rental amount $_____

Delivery/pickup by_____

Return by _____

❧ *Groom's Accessories List*

	Retail Shop	Sales Rep	Size	Cost
Shoes	_____	_____	_____	_____
Underwear	_____	_____	_____	_____
Hosiery	_____	_____	_____	_____
Necktie/ascot	_____	_____	_____	_____
Gloves	_____	_____	_____	_____
Cuff links	_____	_____	_____	_____

Tuxedo Terms

Jackets

May be single-breasted or double-breasted (the latter may look more flattering over a larger stomach)

Lapels

SHAWL: a continuous, slightly curved line from the shoulder to first button

PEAK: narrow, upward cut just below the collar; the lower lapel protrudes beyond the upper

FISHMOUTH (NOTCH): a wider, triangular opening, with the upper and lower lapel the same width

Shirts

COLLARS: stand-up; wing (points fold outward to resemble wings); turn-down

STAYS: stiffening material inserted in the points of collars to hold them in place

FRENCH CUFFS: turn-back cuffs that require cuff links

STUDS: fastenings inserted to close the shirt front when there are no buttons, often in precious materials, such as gold or onyx or diamonds

Shoes

BLACK PATENT LEATHER SLIPPERS (OPERA SLIPPERS): sometimes trimmed with satin

BLACK FORMAL SHOES: very streamlined tie shoes,

Accessories

CUMMERBUND: used to hide any other hardware at the waistline (suspender buttons or clips, for instance); always wear with pleats opening upward

WAISTCOAT/VEST: can be a nice counterpoint to the jacket; alternative to a cummerbund

❧ *Work Sheet for the Best Man's, Groomsmen's/Ushers' Attire*

Retail shop _____   Sales rep _____

Address _____

_____   Phone _____

Tuxedo style _____   Fabric _____   Color _____

Afrocentric style _____   Fabric _____   Color _____

Designer _____   Size _____   Rental cost $ _____

Delivery/pickup by _____

Return by _____

❧

❧ *Best Man's, Groomsmen's/Ushers' Accessories List*

Retail shop _____ Sales rep_____

Address _____

_____ Phone _____

Shoes _____ Size_____ Cost $ _____

Shirt_____ Size_____ Cost $ _____

Necktie/ascot_____ Cost $_____

Gloves_____ Cost $_____

Cuff links_____ Cost $_____

Total cost $ _____

❧ Work Sheet for Fathers' Attire

Retail shop _____ Sales rep_____

Address _____

_____ Phone_____

Tuxedo style _____ Fabric _____ Color _____

Afrocentric style _____ Fabric _____ Color _____

Designer _____ Size _____ Rental cost $ _____

Delivery/pickup by_____

Return by_____

❧ Fathers' Accessories List

Retail shop_____   Sales rep_____

Address _____

_____   Phone_____

Shoes _____   Size_____   Cost $ _____

Shirt_____   Size_____   Cost $ _____

Necktie/ascot_____   Cost $_____

Gloves_____   Cost $_____

Cuff links_____   Cost $_____

Total cost $ _____

You've only begun to shop! Likely, you'll revisit these work sheets over and over again until you make your deposits and even until you have those final fittings. But we believe dressing the part is the best way to envision yourself being there, so now that you know you'll look good wherever you do the "I do," let's get down to planning the ceremony.

**Good planning will make your ceremony as individual as you are.
This couple does their own variation on the candlelighting nuptial ritual.**

Five

YOUR CEREMONY,

YOUR WAY

IMAGINING **WHAT YOU'LL** all wear and shopping for the apparel and accessories that will create your signature look is great fun, especially when the appearance is reflecting a deeply meaningful ceremony of commitment. In this chapter we'll help you plan a ceremony that reflects you and what this rite called marriage means to you.

Look back at your joint vision in chapter I. What setting and style of ceremony did you imagine? What words and rituals and music did you envision as the expression of your love? Whether you saw yourselves exchanging vows under an arbor at an outdoor garden, at the altar in a magnificent cathedral, or in the parlor of an Afrocentric bed-and-breakfast, you can find the location of your dreams and the officiant(s) to help you structure the ceremony that will be most meaningful for you.

FIRST CALLS

Keep the spiritual and emotional factors that are important to you firmly in mind. Then be mindful of your financial resources and the main points of the preliminary plan you established in chapter 3 as you begin the process of finding the perfect ceremony site.

Start by brainstorming for several locations that would suit your vision and also be likely to fit your budget. List them in the Ceremony Sites Possibilities Work Sheet below. (If you live in a city where good locations are in great demand or you have allowed less than a year for planning, your list may need to be longer.)

Call each of the locations to ask whether they're available on your dates of choice, whether they can accommodate the number of people on your guest list, and what fees they charge, if any. Note all the information you gather in the spaces provided in the work sheet.

❧ Ceremony Sites Possibilities

Dates and times of choice_____

Budget _____

Estimated number of guests _____

LOCATION	AVAILABILITY	CAPACITY	COST
1. _____	_____	_____	_____

2. _____   _____   _____   _____

3. _____   _____   _____   _____

4. _____   _____   _____   _____

5. _____   _____   _____   _____

MAKING YOUR DECISION

Once you have two or three locations that meet your criteria for budget, date, and size, you're ready to make an appointment to see the sites. Take a description of your vision with you when you visit, along with a list of questions to ask about the site's facilities and requirements.

- Does the site have an officiant who could perform our wedding ceremony? May we bring in our own instead?

- Does the site provide music? What instruments are available (such as an organ or piano)? May we make our own selections? May we hire outside musicians to supplement or replace the site's musicians?

- May we decorate the site ourselves? Are there restrictions on the use of materials or necessary insurance policies?

- What equipment (such as aisle runners and kneelers) does the site provide?

- May we hold a receiving line at the site? May our guests throw rice or birdseed at the end of the ceremony?

- May our vendors (florist, balloon artist, photographer, wedding consultant) have access to the site before the ceremony? Are there restrictions on taking photography or videography during the ceremony?

- Are there reception facilities? What is the additional cost? Are there any restrictions on dancing or serving food and beverages?

Take a camera with you to snap informal shots of the sites (which you can paste into the space provided below) and record all the answers to your questions in the Ceremony Sites Work Sheet.

❧ *Ceremony Sites Work Sheet*

Budget _____   Wedding date/time _____ / _____

<u>SITE #1</u>   ### <u>SITE #2</u>

Name_____   Name _____

Phone_____   Phone_____

Description_____   Description _____

Cost $_____   Cost $ _____

Ceremony Site

Date available _____   Date available _____

Time available _____   Time available _____

Occupancy _____   Occupancy _____

Rental fee $ _____   Rental fee $ _____

Officiant

Name _____   Name _____

Address_____   Address _____

Phone _____   Phone _____

Fee $_____   Fee $ _____

Music

Organist _____   Organist _____

Soloist _____   Soloist _____

Drummer _____   Drummer _____

Options _____   Options _____

Equipment

Aisle runner _____   Aisle runner _____

Canopy _____   Canopy _____

Kneeler _____   Pillow _____

Altar _____   Altar _____

Other _____   Other _____

Restrictions

Photography _____   Photography _____

Candles _____   Candles _____

Music _____   Music _____

Rice/rose petals _____   Rice/rose petals _____

Miscellaneous Fees

Church sexton _____   Church sexton _____

Total cost $ _____   _____

If you're not going to use the officiant at your ceremony site (or your site doesn't offer one) and you don't already have another officiant in mind, ask friends for recommendations and consult churches or other organizations compatible with your wedding vision. Your local Marriage License Bureau should be able to refer you to judges and magistrates who are qualified to perform weddings if you're having a civil ceremony.

Use the work sheet below to keep notes as you interview possible officiants. Be sure to ask not only about his or her availability on your dates of choice, but also about what documents and counseling sessions might be required.

❧ Officiant Work Sheet

Officiant #1

Title and name _____

Religious/spiritual affiliation _____

Address _____

Phone _____

Availability _____

Fees _____

Requirements _____

Officiant #2

Title and name _____

Religious/spiritual affiliation _____

Address _____

Phone _____

Availability _____

Fees _____

Requirements _____

Use this space for additional notes as you interview possible officiants

Place business card here

Place business card here

Once you've decided on your ceremony site and officiant(s), you can use the Wedding Reservation Checklist here to make a record of all the names and addresses, equipment, and requirements. (The elements and plan for your ceremony itself come next.) We've included space for your reception in this work sheet, too, in case you'll be holding it at the same location.

✒ Wedding Reservation Checklist

Wedding

Date _____ Time _____

Style of wedding ☐ Afrocentric ☐ Traditional ☐ Formal ☐ Semi-Formal ☐ Informal

Number of guests _____

Number of attendants _____

Bride _____ Bridegroom _____

Other Attendants

Flower girl(s) _____ Ring bearer(s) _____ Train bearer(s) _____

Hosts _____ Hostesses _____

Color scheme _____

Officiant _____ Phone _____

Counseling session requirements _____

Dates _____ Time _____

Location _____

Ceremony Site

Phone _____

Address _____

Restrictions_____

Special requirements _____

Equipment needed_____

Decorating ideas _____

_____

Rehearsal date _____Time _____

Fee $_____

Reception Site

Phone _____

Address _____

Reception site reserved

From_____until _____

Cocktail hour room _____Dining room_____

Capacity _____

Restrictions_____

Special requirements _____

Equipment needed_____

_____

Decorating ideas _____

_____

Fee $_____

Comments _____

_____

_____

Premarital counseling is an important part of many spiritual traditions. In Africa, a wedding is a community event—extending old ties and creating new ones—and the couple's preparation reflects the concerns and experience of the larger society. The bride-to-be in many African cultures meets with elder women and the groom-to-be with the elder men for instruction and guidance. Many Christian denominations and other religious faiths have similar practices. If your officiant of choice advises counseling, use the session to receive the wisdom of your elders and guides, whatever tradition you embrace.

THE ORDER OF SERVICE

Once you've decided on your ceremony site and your officiant(s), you're ready to plan the order of service for your ceremony. Make an appointment with your officiant to discuss the standard order of service he or she follows and ways that you might add to it or modify it to make it more your own.

Do your homework before your meeting. That is, really think about and discuss what will make your ceremony the embodiment of what you feel for one another and the commitment you are making. You may feel as though the traditional service—the one your parents and grandparents were married by—is the right one for you. Even so, you may want to give your friends and families opportunities to participate by reading prayers or scriptures or special pieces of literature. Perhaps you'd like to include Afrocentric rituals or personalize your ceremony by writing your own vows. Prepare a list of your ideas and be sure to ask your officiant for suggestions. Below is a Ceremony Work Sheet that outlines the key elements of most wedding services, regardless of tradition, and gives you a place to write *your* order of service, including readings and other rituals, as well as a place to assign roles to special participants.

❧ *Ceremony Work Sheet*

TRADITIONAL ORDER OF SERVICE	OUR ORDER OF SERVICE	PARTICIPANTS
The Charge to the Congregation (to act as witnesses)	_____	_____
The Charge to the Bride and Groom (to ask if there is any reason they cannot be married)	_____	_____
The Declaration of Intent (to be sure the couple understands the vows they are about to take)	_____	_____
The Exchange of Vows	_____	_____
The Exchange of Rings	_____	_____
The Pronouncement (to declare the couple husband and wife)	_____	_____
Readings	_____	_____
	_____	_____
	_____	_____
Other rituals	_____	_____
	_____	_____
	_____	_____

Afrocentric Ceremony Rituals

Pouring of a Libation. In many African cultures, ancestors are considered always present, guarding and guiding the lives of their descendants. The ritual pouring of a libation during the wedding ceremony symbolically invites the ancestors to witness and give their blessing to the occasion.

Tasting of Four Elements (also called Bitter Herb Tasting). This ritual employs four elements or herbs—one bitter, one sour, one hot, and one sweet—to represent the ups and downs of marriage. The couple tastes each one in succession, coming at last to the sweetness that grows out of meeting all of life's challenges, the good and the bad, together.

Exchange of Kola Nuts. An African symbol of healing, the kola nut represents the couple's ability to resolve and overcome differences in their relationship. Some brides and grooms choose to exchange kola nuts after they exchange vows to symbolize the strength of their commitment.

Jumping the Broom. The custom of jumping the broom may have originated in Africa, where brooms were thought to bring spiritual as well as physical cleanliness. During the time of slavery in America, when African-Americans' marriages were not recognized by the law, couples jumped the broom to show that they were making a home together and to "sweep away" any evil influences.

Your vows are at the heart of your wedding ceremony, the moment when you pledge your commitment to each other in the presence of all those you've asked as loving witnesses. More and more couples are using their own words to express the promise they're making, to say more about themselves as individuals and of the lives they're joining together, including children they may be bringing into the marriage. The traditional words "I take thee . . . to have and to hold, from this day forward, for better or worse," as they have been spoken through the centuries, may be the perfect expression of this great moment for you and your fiancé. Even if that's the case, you may want to use the Vows Work Sheet to write down what the commitment of marriage means to you and why each of you has chosen the other "to love and to cherish, till death us do part."

Vows Work Sheet

🕊 Bride's 🕊

_____

_____

_____

_____

_____

🕊 Groom's 🕊

_____

_____

_____

_____

_____

The music you select for your ceremony can say as much as the words. The language of African talking drums may create the atmosphere you want for your wedding better than the sounds of the traditional Wedding March. If you're like most couples of African descent, you enjoy a wide variety of music, and the two of you will need to sit down together and discuss the kinds of music that will best accompany and enhance the style of ceremony you've planned. (Some churches will not allow secular music because they believe a wedding service is a worship service, so be sure to check with your officiant about any restrictions that may apply.)

If your site has a musical director, your next order of business is to meet with him or her to go over your preferences and get suggestions. If you want to bring in other musicians or vocalists, be sure to ask about the proper protocol. (See chapter 6 for tips on hiring musicians.)

The following Ceremony Music Work Sheet lists the traditional musical elements of a wedding and provides space to write in your selections and show who will be playing them.

❧ *Ceremony Music List*

	PIECE	ORGANIST	OTHER MUSICIANS	CHOIR/ SOLOIST
Prelude				
Processional				
Hymns				
Songs				
Recessional				
Postlude				
Receiving line music				

After you've planned your order of service and chosen the music, you have the information you need to compose a wedding program that can be used as a guide for participants and guests and saved as a memento of your Big Day.

Use the work sheet below to be sure you've covered all the details, including the names of the wedding party and explanations of any special rituals you're including. Your site may be able to print your program, or you can add it as another element when you order your wedding invitations. (See chapter 10.) In either case, try to make sure it complements the style of your other printed pieces.

❧ Wedding Program Work Sheet

The name of the bride _____

The name of the bridegroom _____

The names of the bride's parents _____

The names of the bridegroom's parents _____

Date and time of the ceremony _____

Location of the ceremony_____

Style of ceremony _____

Order of service _____

Titles of musical selections _____

_____

Names of the Members of the Wedding Party

Bride's Attendants

Honor attendants _____

_____

Bridesmaids _____

_____

_____

_____

Junior bridesmaids _____

_____

_____

_____

Flower girls _____

_____

_____

Train bearers _____

_____

Bridegroom's Attendants

Best man _____

Groomsmen _____

_____

_____

Head usher _____

Ushers _____

_____

_____

_____

Junior ushers _____

_____

_____

Ring bearer _____

Pages _____

_____

Name(s) of the Officiant(s)

_____

_____

Names of the Musicians

Organist _____

Choir _____

_____

_____

Soloists _____

_____

_____

Other musicians _____

_____

_____

Additional copy _____

_____

_____

_____

Ill the participants in the ceremony—including musicians who will be playing during the processional and recessional—should gather at the site for a rehearsal at least a day ahead of time. Your officiant or wedding consultant will preside and make sure everyone knows what to do when, from seating guests to forming a receiving line after the ceremony.

Seating. During the rehearsal, the ushers will receive instructions on how to stand while awaiting the arrival of guests, how to greet and escort them, and where to seat them. The bride's family and friends are traditionally ushered to seats on the left side of the aisle (the bride's side) and the groom's family and friends to seats on the right side (the groom's side). Immediate family members usually occupy a reserved section on the appropriate side at the front of the site, within the ribbons, if the ceremony is being held in a church. (See chapter 10 for ordering within-the-ribbons cards to enclose in the invitations of those who will have reserved seating.) The mothers of the bride and groom are the last to be seated, just before the ceremony begins.

Plan the details of your seating arrangement before the rehearsal using the following guidelines for both the bride's and the groom's side:

- **Pew 1:** Mother and father (or divorced mother and her husband, if she has remarried)
- **Pew 2:** Grandparents; sisters and spouses (with children, if invited); brothers and spouses (with children, if invited); godparents of the bride (optional)
- **Pew 3:** Divorced father and his wife, aunts, uncles, and cousins
- **Pew 4:** Other relatives and close friends

❧ Ceremony Seating List

❧ *Bride's Side* ❧

Pew 1 _____

_____

_____

Pew 2 _____

_____

_____

Pew 3 _____

_____

_____

Pew 4 _____

_____

_____

Bridegroom's Side

Pew 1 _____

_____

_____

Pew 2 _____

_____

_____

Pew 3 _____

_____

_____

Pew 4 _____

_____

_____

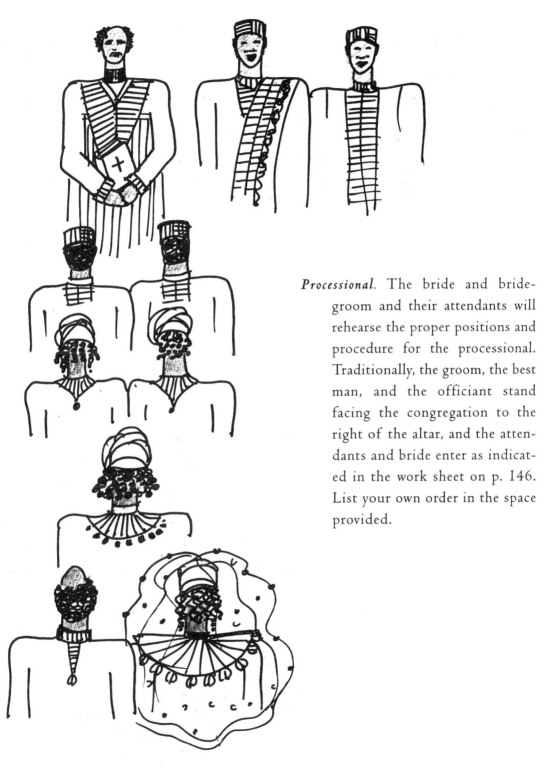

Processional. The bride and bridegroom and their attendants will rehearse the proper positions and procedure for the processional. Traditionally, the groom, the best man, and the officiant stand facing the congregation to the right of the altar, and the attendants and bride enter as indicated in the work sheet on p. 146. List your own order in the space provided.

A Work Sheet for the Processional

TRADITIONAL ORDER	**OUR ORDER**
The groomsmen	______________________
The bridesmaids	______________________
The junior bridesmaids	______________________
The maid/matron of honor	______________________
The ring bearer	______________________
The flower girl(s)	______________________
The bride and her father	______________________
The train bearers	______________________

Positions During the Ceremony. Members of the wedding party remain in the positions at which they arrived at the altar at the end of the processional, except for the honor attendants who administer to the couple. Below is an illustration of the traditional positions at the altar.

❧ Traditional Positions ❧

The Altar

The Officiant(s)

Bridesmaids   Maid/Matron of Honor   Bride and Groom   Best Man   Groomsmen

Junior Bridesmaids   Flower Girl(s)   Ring Bearer   Junior Groomsman

The Recessional. After the officiant pronounces you husband and wife, you kiss. Hallelujah! Then the two of you and the bridal party turn in your places to start the recessional. This ceremonial exit is led by you newlyweds, immediately followed by the wedding party in pairs (honor attendant with the best man, junior attendants and each bridesmaid with a groomsman), and then followed by the bride's parents and the groom's parents. (If there are extra male or female attendants, they may pair up with each other.)

The Receiving Line. You may wish to run through your plans for a receiving line during the rehearsal, too, if you plan to form one at the ceremony site. With the help of your officiant or wedding consultant, choose the best area for the line, and use the traditional guidelines at right to set up your own order. If your wedding is formal and very large, it can be helpful to assign an announcer who stands next to the mother of the bride. He asks each guest their name as they approach the line and repeats the name to the mother of the bride, who will then introduce them to the mother of the bridegroom.

🍂 *A Work Sheet for the Receiving Line*

TRADITIONAL ORDER	OUR ORDER
(Announcer)	_____
Mother of the bride	_____
Father of the bride (optional)	_____
Mother of the bridegroom	_____
Father of the bridegroom (optional)	_____
Bride	_____
Bridegroom	_____
Best man (optional)	_____
Maid/matron of honor	_____
Bridesmaid (optional)	_____
Bridesmaid (optional)	_____
Bridesmaid (optional)	_____

Ask everyone who's involved in the ceremony to attend the rehearsal and to be on time. (And ask your bridesmaids to bring their wedding shoes so that you can match partners for the recessional according to height.) Use the following checklist to keep track of the rehearsal participants and the elements rehearsed.

❧ Rehearsal Checklist

Participants

NAME	PHONE

Key Items Rehearsed

❏ Bridesmaids and groomsmen paired

❏ Head usher assigned and instructed on reserving pews for family

❏ Ushers instructed on greeting and seating guests

❏ Ushers instructed on seating latecomers

❏ Honor ushers for mothers assigned

❏ Ushers informed of time they are expected to arrive at wedding

❏ Children's roles walked through

❏ Processional walked through

❏ Recessional walked through

❏ Receiving line arranged

❏ Announcer assigned, if needed

A rehearsal album of well-wishers for the bride and groom

Maid of honor

Best man

Head Usher

Announcer

Child Attendant

Child Attendant

A rehearsal album of well-wishers for the bride and groom

Bridesmaid

_____
_____
_____

Bridesmaid

_____
_____
_____

Bridesmaid

_____
_____
_____

Bridesmaid

_____
_____
_____

Bridesmaid

_____
_____
_____

Bridesmaid

_____
_____
_____

A rehearsal album of well-wishers for the bride and groom

Groomsman

Groomsman

Groomsman

Groomsman

Groomsman

Groomsman

A rehearsal album of well-wishers for the bride and groom

Usher

_____

_____

_____

_____

Usher

_____

_____

_____

_____

Usher

_____

_____

_____

_____

Usher

_____

_____

_____

_____

Usher

_____

_____

_____

_____

Usher

_____

_____

_____

_____

I t is the bride's responsibility, with the help of the best man, to arrange transportation for her attendants, the immediate families, and other special guests to the ceremony site and then on to the reception. (Don't forget elderly relatives and friends who may also need arrangements.) The best man arranges transportation for the out-of-town guests (if they do not have cars) from the airport to the hotels, to the church and reception sites, and back to the hotels and airport or train stations for their final departure.

First determine how many people will need transportation and where they will be picked up. Then hire the necessary number of vehicles. Some couples are choosing buses, vans, trolleys, horse-drawn carriages, horse-drawn sleighs (in the wintertime), boats or gondolas (if you have a waterside ceremony site), so be limited only by your joint vision (and budget!). The traditional groupings for transportation are:

- The bride, her father (or whoever will be escorting her up the aisle), and the maid/matron of honor
- The bride's mother and the bridesmaids
- The groom and his best man (groomsmen and ushers arrange their own)
- The groom's family

It's the best man's duty to transport the couple to the airport for their honeymoon, but if your budget allows, you might consider renting a limousine instead.

Use the Transportation Work Sheet at right to identify the kind of service that will fit your budget. Once you decide on transportation, note the details in the Transportation Contract Checklist.

❧ *Transportation Work Sheet*

Budget: $ _____   Wedding Date/Time: _____ / _____

Company #1

Company _____   Contact person _____

Address _____

Phone_____   Beeper_____

Cost per hour $ _____   Amount of hours _____   Overtime rate per hour $_____

No. of vehicles_____   Type of vehicles _____   Capacity _____

_____   _____   _____

Amenities included _____

_____

Company #2

Company _____   Contact person _____

Address _____

Phone_____   Beeper_____

Cost per hour $ _____   Amount of hours _____   Overtime rate per hour $_____

No. of vehicles_____   Type of vehicles _____   Capacity _____

_____   _____   _____

Amenities included _____

_____

Company #3

Company _____   Contact person _____

Address _____

Phone_____   Beeper_____

Cost per hour $ _____   Amount of hours _____   Overtime rate per hour $_____

No. of vehicles_____   Type of vehicles _____   Capacity _____

_____   _____   _____

Amenities included _____

_____

Company #4

Company _____   Contact person _____

Address _____

Phone_____   Beeper_____

Cost per hour $ _____   Amount of hours _____   Overtime rate per hour $_____

No. of vehicles_____   Type of vehicles _____   Capacity _____

_____   _____   _____

Amenities included _____

_____

🕊 *Transportation Contract Checklist*

Company _____ Contact _____

Address _____

Phone _____ Beeper _____

Wedding date _____ Time _____

Wedding site/address _____ / _____

Reception site/address _____ / _____

No. of vehicles _____ Cost per hour $_____ Overtime rate per hour $_____

No. of hours _____ Date of contract _____

Total cost $_____ Deposit $_____ Date of deposit _____

Balance due $_____ Date of balance due _____

Other _____

Vehicle #1

Model _____ Description _____

Seating capacity _____ Driver _____

PICKUP LOCATION	TIME	CEREMONY ARRIVAL TIME	RECEPTION SITE ARRIVAL TIME
_____	_____	_____	_____
Passengers _____	_____	_____	
_____	_____	_____	
_____	_____	_____	

Amenities_____

Cost $ _____

Vehicle #2

Model_____   Description _____

Seating capacity_____   Driver _____

PICKUP LOCATION	**TIME**	**CEREMONY ARRIVAL TIME**	**RECEPTION SITE ARRIVAL TIME**
_____	_____	_____	_____
Passengers _____	_____		_____
_____	_____		_____
_____	_____		_____

Amenities_____

Cost $ _____

Vehicle #3

Model_____   Description _____

Seating capacity_____   Driver _____

PICKUP LOCATION	**TIME**	**CEREMONY ARRIVAL TIME**	**RECEPTION SITE ARRIVAL TIME**
_____	_____	_____	_____
Passengers _____	_____		_____

_____ _____ _____

_____ _____ _____

Amenities_____

Cost $ _____

Vehicle #4

Model_____   Description _____

Seating capacity_____   Driver _____

PICKUP LOCATION	**TIME**	**CEREMONY ARRIVAL TIME**	**RECEPTION SITE ARRIVAL TIME**
_____	_____	_____	_____
Passengers _____	_____		_____
_____	_____		_____
_____	_____		_____

Amenities_____

Cost $ _____

THE WEDDING DAY SCHEDULE

Planning your wedding day schedule and putting it in writing will provide a useful tool for the person that you select as *supervisor of the day*. Once the two of you have decided who's going to do what on your *Big Day*, fill in the Wedding Day Schedule provided to help you organize the day. Include the names and phone numbers of your vendors, what they are to deliver, when and where (your home, wedding site, reception site), and who will receive the delivery.

❧ *Wedding Day Schedule Checklist*

TIME	VENDOR
_____	_____
_____	_____
_____	_____
_____	_____
_____	_____
_____	_____
_____	_____
_____	_____
_____	_____
_____	_____
_____	_____
_____	_____

DELIVERY LOCATION	CONTACT	PHONE

Receptions are all about celebration!

Six

PLANNING YOUR CELEBRATION:

THE RECEPTION

O NCE YOU'VE TAKEN your solemn vows, you'll want to celebrate! This chapter is designed to help you enjoy the festivities of making your big commitment with those who
have gathered to witness and support you, without a single worry. Whether you feel the
most appropriate celebration is a quiet cake-and-coffee tribute to the sacredness of the
occasion or a party that makes a "joyful noise," you have a rich and varied heritage from
which to express what's in your hearts. From African dance and drumming to Caribbean

feasting and music-making, or from steamy jazz and Southern barbecue to traditional hymns and scripture showers, you can say "celebrate" in many cultures and styles.

Where you celebrate will do much to set the tone and atmosphere. Church hall, hotel ballroom, country club, restaurant, or private home—take the time to find the best location for your vision as well as your finances.

Styles of Reception

Breakfast Reception. Generally smaller (50 to 75 guests) and less formal than an evening reception, breakfast receptions can range from cozy homestyle feasts of biscuits and grits to elegant omelettes and croissants. Raise your glasses of mimosas and make an early start on married life!

Brunch or Lunch. Usually about the same size as a breakfast reception and about the same degree of formality, brunch or lunch receptions tend to include midday fare such as salads and sandwiches.

Cocktail Reception. 50 or more guests, informal to formal. Cocktails and hors d'oeuvres may be the perfect solution for those who want the sophistication of an evening celebration without the expense of a full meal. Two or three hours (instead of the usual four to six), still allows plenty of time for dancing, toasting, and cutting the cake.

Evening Reception. 50 or more guests, informal to formal. About 95 percent of all couples still opt for the evening reception. You can keep costs down by having serving stations and buffets rather than a seated meal and by limiting the cocktail hour or serving only wine and beer—and champagne for the Big Toast, of course.

f you'll be holding your reception in a separate location from your ceremony, you'll first need to make a short list of possibilities and contact each of them to determine capacity, availability, and cost. Use the work sheet below to keep track of the information you gather:

❧ *Reception Site Possibilities Work Sheet*

Dates and times of choice_____

Budget $_____

Estimated no. of guests _____

	LOCATION	AVAILABILITY	CAPACITY	COST PER PERSON
1.				
2.				
3.				
4.				
5.				

Once you've found two or three places that suit your style and budget, make appointments to visit the sites and meet with the management. Any banquet facility will have an experienced staff who can handle just about any request and coordinate your reception schedule. Go to your appointment prepared with a detailed description of the reception you envision and a list of questions about the services the facility provides:

- What menu options do they offer? Do they hold tasting sessions?
- Will they make the wedding cake?
- Is the bar service unlimited, or do they charge per person?
- What is their usual length of reception? Are there overtime fees?
- Are there restrictions on decorating, music, or other use of the space?
- Are there parking facilities? Is the cost included or additional?

If you decide to have your reception in a private home or a location that doesn't offer food service and you'll be hiring a caterer, you'll need to ask the caterer about menu options as well as about rental fees for dishes, flatware, crystal, tables, chairs, tablecloths, and napkins. If they charge a flat fee for the entire catering service, ask what their fee would be for food alone, excluding the other items, so that you can decide whether to supply those items yourselves. Use the Reception Site Work Sheet below to record and organize the information for each site (or caterer) and to help you make your final choice.

Reception Site Work Sheet

Our budget $_____

Style _____ Number of guests _____

Reception date _____ Time: From _____ to _____

Reception Site #1

Location _____

Banquet manager _____

Address _____

Phone _____ Fax _____

Date available _____ Time available _____

Cocktail hour room _____ Dining room _____

Capacity _____ Color scheme _____

Services _____

_____

Restrictions _____

Equipment needed _____

Rental fee $ _____

Cost per person: Food $ _____ Beverages $ _____

Gratuities $ _____ Tax $ _____ Total cost $ _____

Cancellation policy _____

Reception Site #2

Location _____

Banquet manager _____

Address _____

Phone _____ Fax _____

Date available_____   Time available_____

Cocktail hour room _____   Dining room _____

Capacity _____   Color scheme_____

Services _____

_____

Restrictions _____

Equipment needed_____

Rental fee $ _____

Cost per person: Food $_____   Beverages $_____

Gratuities $_____   Tax $_____   Total cost $_____

Cancellation policy _____

Reception Site #3

Location _____

Banquet manager _____

Address _____

Phone_____   Fax _____

Date available_____   Time available_____

Cocktail hour room _____   Dining room _____

Capacity _____   Color scheme_____

Services _____

_____

Restrictions _____

Equipment needed _____

Rental fee $ _____

Cost per person: Food $ _____ Beverages $ _____

Gratuities $_____ Tax $_____ Total cost $ _____

Cancellation policy _____

THE CONTRACT

Once you've found the site that best suits your vision, your budget, and your needs, be sure to get all the terms of your agreement in a signed and counter-signed contract. The checklist below will help you keep track of every important detail.

❧ *Reception Site Contract Checklist*

Contract date _____

Site name _____

Address _____

Banquet manager _____ Maître d'hôtel _____

Phone_____ Fax _____

Reception date _____ Time: From _____to_____

Cocktail hour room _____ Dining room _____

Cocktail menu _____

Liquor Package

Premium brands_____   Cash bar: yes ❏ no ❏ Number of hours _____

Number of food stations _____   Describe_____

Dinner menu

Appetizers _____

_____

Meats/fish/main dishes _____

_____

Side dishes _____

_____

Breads _____

_____

Salads _____

_____

Desserts_____

_____

Wedding cake(s) (describe decorations)

Bride's_____   Number of tiers_____   Number of servings_____

Groom's_____   Number of layers_____   Number of servings_____

Style of reception ☐ Afrocentric ☐ Formal ☐ Semi-Formal ☐ Informal

Number of attendants _____ Number of guests _____

Type of Reception ☐ Sit-down ☐ Buffet ☐ Cocktails/hors d'oeuvres

Caterer (when held in private home or location with no on-site catering staff)

Contact person _____ Phone _____

Confirmed date _____ Time _____

Services _____

_____

Decorating ideas _____

Restrictions _____

Special requirements _____

Equipment needed _____

Rental fee $ _____

Cost per person:

Food $ _____ Beverage $ _____

Gratuities $_____ Tax $_____ Total cost $_____

Cancellation policy _____

Terms of Payment

Deposit amount $ _____ Date due_____

Balance $_____ Date due_____

Deadline date for final head count_____

Total number confirmed _____

Choosing the right music to dine by, the right music to dance to, the music that will create the atmosphere you've envisioned and that all your guests can enjoy, takes careful thought and planning. Begin by using Our Favorite Tunes Work Sheet to identify your and your fiancé's preferences in styles of music and to list the special songs you want to include, imagining which ones would best accompany each part of your reception. (Be sure you've asked at your site whether there are any restrictions that will affect your choices.)

❧ Our Favorite Tunes

	SELECTION	ARTIST
Receiving line	_____	_____
	_____	_____
	_____	_____
	_____	_____
	_____	_____
Cocktail hour	_____	_____
	_____	_____
	_____	_____
	_____	_____
Meal	_____	_____
	_____	_____

Toasts   _____   _____

First dance   _____   _____

Cutting the cake _____   _____

Bouquet toss _____   _____

Garter toss _____   _____

_____   _____

_____   _____

_____   _____

Other (specify) _____   _____

_____   _____

_____   _____

_____   _____

LIVE MUSIC OR DJ, COMBO OR QUARTET?

After you've compiled the list of your favorite tunes, discuss how you'd most like to hear them played. Do you imagine a jazz combo or classical quartet providing background music at your breakfast or brunch reception? Do you want a live band with a versatile repertoire that can play a soft romantic piece as guests go through the receiving line and then shift gears for a dance party after dinner? Do you want drummers who can add a ceremonial African beat to your celebration? Or do you want to hear the old Motown standards in their original versions, spun by a DJ who can also act as a master of ceremonies? Maybe you'd even like to combine live and recorded music.

Gather recommendations of musicians and DJs from your friends. Consult the *Yellow Pages* or the *Black Pages* under "Bands and Orchestras" and "Entertainers." Be sure to meet all the musicians or DJs you're considering and see them perform (or get videotapes of their work). Show them your list of tunes and ask for their suggestions. The Reception Music Work Sheet here will help you compare the different possibilities for both bands and DJs you investigate.

❧ *Reception Music Work Sheet*

Our Budget $ _____

Band Possibility #1

Audition date _____   Time _____

Name of band/muscians _____

Style _____

Contact _____

Address _____

Phone _____   Fax _____

Name of band leader _____

Piano/keyboard _____

Singers _____   _____

Drummer _____   Bass _____

Saxophone _____   Trumpet _____

Others (names of backup performers and instruments) _____

_____

_____

_____

Equipment _____

Total number of musicians _____   Number of breaks _____

Cost $_____   Overtime fees (per hr.) $ _____

Cancellation policy _____

Comments _____

Band Possibility #2

Audition date_____ Time _____

Name of band/muscians _____

Style _____

Contact _____

Address _____

Phone_____ Fax _____

Name of band leader_____

Piano/keyboard _____

Singers _____   _____

Drummer_____ Bass _____

Saxophone _____ Trumpet _____

Others (names of backup performers and instruments) _____

_____

_____

_____

Equipment _____

Total number of musicians_____ Number of breaks _____

Cost $_____ Overtime fees (per hr.) $ _____

Cancellation policy _____

Comments _____

Band Possibility #3

Audition date_____ Time _____

Name of band/muscians _____

Style _____

Contact _____

Address _____

Phone_____ Fax _____

Name of band leader_____

Piano/keyboard _____

Singers _____ _____

Drummer_____ Bass_____

Saxophone _____ Trumpet _____

Others (names of backup performers and instruments) _____

_____

_____

_____

Equipment _____

Total number of musicians_____ Number of breaks _____

Cost $_____ Overtime fees (per hr.) $ _____

Cancellation policy _____

Comments _____

DJ Possibility #1

Audition date_____ Time _____

Disc jockey (DJ)_____

Style _____

Contact _____

Address _____

Phone_____ Fax _____

Equipment _____

Number of people to work_____

Cost $_____ Overtime fees (per hr.) $ _____

Cancellation policy _____

Comments _____

DJ Possibility #2

Audition date_____ Time _____

Disc jockey (DJ)_____

Style _____

Contact _____

Address _____

Phone_____ Fax _____

Equipment _____

Number of people to work_____

Cost $_____   Overtime fees (per hr.) $ _____

Cancellation policy _____

Comments _____

DJ Possibility #3

Audition date_____   Time _____

Disc jockey (DJ)_____

Style _____

Contact _____

Address _____

Phone_____   Fax _____

Equipment _____

Number of people to work_____

Cost $_____   Overtime fees (per hr.) $ _____

Cancellation policy _____

Comments _____

When you've decided on the musicians or DJ or combination, get the deal in writing in all its particulars, with the signatures of all the principal parties, not just the manager:

❧ *Music Contract*

Event date _____ Contract date _____

Band/muscians/DJ _____

Contact _____

Address _____

Phone _____ Fax _____

Arrival time _____ Departure time _____

Number of hours _____

Number of breaks _____ Length of breaks _____

Meal break (type of menu) _____

Cost $ _____ Overtime fees (per hr.) $ _____

Names of performers _____

Name of band leader _____

Piano/keyboard _____

Singers _____ _____

Drummer _____ Bass _____

Saxophone _____ Trumpet _____

Others (names of backup performers and instruments) _____

_____

_____

Equipment _____

Total number of musicians _____

Performers' insurance_____

Terms of payment _____

Deposit amount $ _____   Date due _____

Balance $_____   Date due _____

Cancellation policy _____

_____

Receiving Line. If you're going to hold your receiving line at your reception site, see chapter 5, p. 149 for a work sheet to help you arrange the order of participants.

Seating Arrangements. How you seat your wedding party and your guests at your reception can ensure that everyone has a good time and that the celebration is lively. Give thought to assignments that will keep conversation and good spirits flowing. In the work sheet below, you will see the traditional groupings for the head table and parents' table to use as guidelines when you plan your own arrangements. (Some couples today are choosing to sit at a "sweetheart table" for themselves alone and to seat the bridal party with their significant others.) The youngest children in the wedding party—flower girls, ring bearers, and train bearers—are usually seated with their parents, who can attend to their needs. You can arrange with the banquet manager to set up a separate table, close to the head table, for the junior bridesmaids and junior groomsmen.

❧ *Seating Arrangements*

Type of tables_____   No. of seats at each table _____

Head Table—Bridal Party

Bride and groom

Maid/matron of honor and best man

Bridesmaids and groomsmen

_____

_____

_____

_____

_____

_____

_____

_____

_____

Table 1—Parents' Table

Mother and father of the bride

Mother and father of the groom

Grandparents of bride and groom

Godparents (if possible)

Minister and spouse

_____

_____

_____

_____

_____

_____

_____

_____

Table 2—Family Table

Sisters and brothers of the bride and groom

and children (if invited)

_____

_____

_____

_____

_____

_____

_____

Table 3—Family Table

Close relatives of the bride and groom

_____

_____

_____

_____

_____

_____

_____

_____

Table 4—Family Table

Close relatives of the bride and groom

_____

_____

_____

_____

Table 5—Family Table

Relatives of the bride and groom

_____

_____

_____

_____

_____

_____

_____

_____

_____

_____

Table 6—Family Table

Relatives of the bride and groom

_____

_____

_____

_____

_____

_____

_____

_____

_____

_____

Table 7

Friends

_____

_____

_____

_____

_____

_____

_____

_____

_____

_____

Table 8

Friends

_____

_____

_____

_____

_____

_____

_____

_____

_____

_____

_____

Plan your seating arrangement using this simple line illustration for tables and assignments.
Photocopy the following pages as many times as you need to.

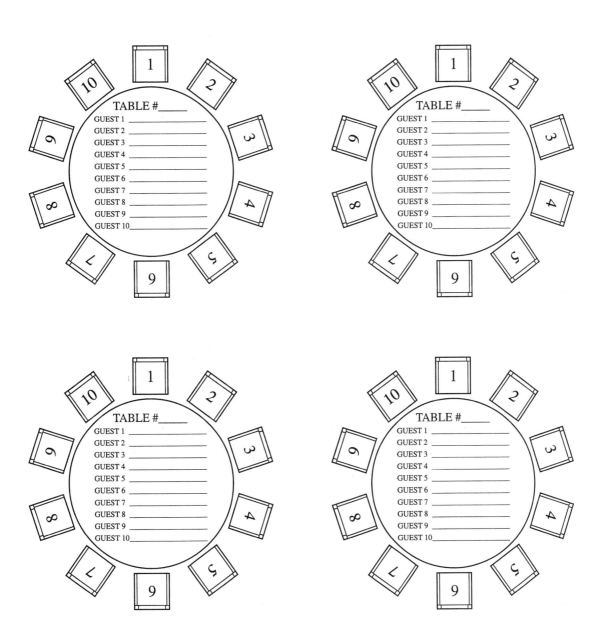

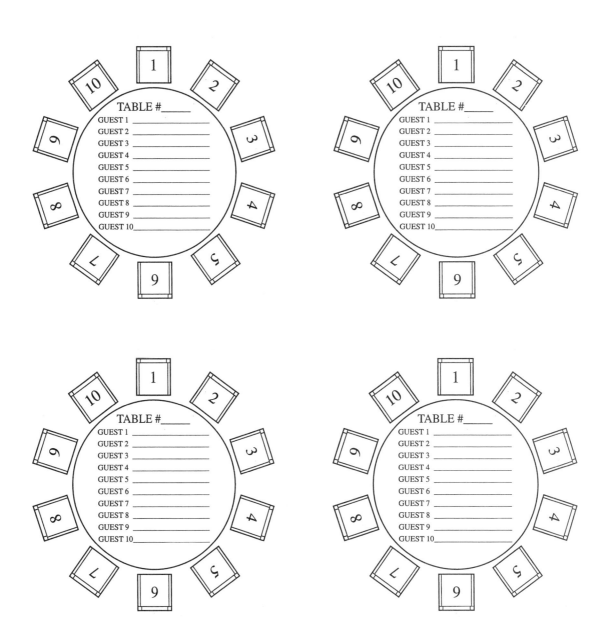

TABLE #_____
GUEST 1 _____
GUEST 2 _____
GUEST 3 _____
GUEST 4 _____
GUEST 5 _____
GUEST 6 _____
GUEST 7 _____
GUEST 8 _____
GUEST 9 _____
GUEST 10_____

TABLE #_____
GUEST 1 _____
GUEST 2 _____
GUEST 3 _____
GUEST 4 _____
GUEST 5 _____
GUEST 6 _____
GUEST 7 _____
GUEST 8 _____
GUEST 9 _____
GUEST 10_____

TABLE #_____
GUEST 1 _____
GUEST 2 _____
GUEST 3 _____
GUEST 4 _____
GUEST 5 _____
GUEST 6 _____
GUEST 7 _____
GUEST 8 _____
GUEST 9 _____
GUEST 10_____

TABLE #_____
GUEST 1 _____
GUEST 2 _____
GUEST 3 _____
GUEST 4 _____
GUEST 5 _____
GUEST 6 _____
GUEST 7 _____
GUEST 8 _____
GUEST 9 _____
GUEST 10_____

Do consider asking willing (and reliable) friends and relatives to act as hosts and hostesses to help keep your reception running smoothly, especially if you haven't hired a wedding consultant. Their duty is to make certain *every* guest is received warmly and is comfortable during the event; as such, they are extensions of the bride's mother, who is the official hostess. If there are any complaints, the head host and hostess can be called upon to handle the matter in a pleasant and efficient manner, leaving the bride and groom and the bride's mother free to enjoy their day. Amelia Montgomery of Weddings by Amelia recommends selecting one host/hostess for every twenty-five guests.

The hosts and hostesses work in conjunction with the wedding consultant, if you *do* hire one, to greet guests, offer directions to rest rooms, elevators, and stairs, receive and safeguard gifts brought to the reception, make sure everyone signs the guest book, and attend to any other needs or requests. At the end of the reception, they assist the ushers in removing gifts from the reception site to the car(s) for transport to the home of the bride and groom.

❧ *Hosts and Hostesses Work Sheet*

Name _____ Phone _____

Address _____

Head host ❑   Head hostess ❑   Host ❑   Hostess ❑

Duties_____

_____

_____

Ceremony site_____ Arrival time_____

Reception site_____ Arrival time_____

Name _____ Phone _____

Address _____

Head host ❏   Head hostess ❏   Host ❏   Hostess ❏

Duties _____

_____

_____

Ceremony site _____ Arrival time _____

Reception site _____ Arrival time _____

Name _____ Phone _____

Address _____

Head host ❏   Head hostess ❏   Host ❏   Hostess ❏

Duties _____

_____

_____

Ceremony site _____ Arrival time _____

Reception site _____ Arrival time _____

Jumping the broom is a great way to make an entrance to your reception.

A RECEPTION SCHEDULE

It's wise to establish a schedule for your reception so that you can be sure to include all the special events you've planned and the traditions you want to observe, as well as to allow time for eating and toasting and dancing (and to avoid overtime fees).

Wedding receptions generally last from three to six hours. We've given you a sample schedule for a six-hour evening reception, which you can adjust according to your style and timetable:

Sample Reception Schedule

5:00–5:55 P.M.	Cocktails and hors d'oeuvres Crystal Room, Club 245
5:55–6:15 P.M.	Guests proceed to ballroom to be seated Imperial Ballroom Hostesses at table to distribute escort cards with assigned table numbers
6:15–6:30 P.M.	Introduction of bridal party Guests go through receiving line, photos are taken
6:30–6:45 P.M.	Bride and groom's first dance Bridal party seated
6:45–7:30 P.M.	The toasts are presented, libations performed, first course is served, dancing begins
8:00 P.M.	The entrée is served, soft music is played
9:00 P.M.	The cake is cut, the bouquet and the garter are tossed, coffee and dessert are served, the bride and groom circulate among their guests, dancing begins
10:00 P.M.	The bride and groom leave at this point, if they do not plan to stay for the entire event
11:00 P.M.	The last dance is played, the parents (and the bride and groom) say goodbye to the guests.

Reception ends

Here's a work sheet to use as you plan your own reception program:

❧ *Order of Events*

Time_____   Event_____

Place_____

Comments_____

_____

Time_____   Event_____

Place_____

Comments_____

_____

Time_____   Event_____

Place_____

Comments_____

_____

Time_____   Event_____

Place_____

Comments_____

_____

Time _____ Event _____

Place _____

Comments _____

_____

Time _____ Event _____

Place _____

Comments _____

_____

Time _____ Event _____

Place _____

Comments _____

_____

Time _____ Event _____

Place _____

Comments _____

_____

Time _____ Event _____

Place _____

Comments _____

_____

Time _____ Event _____

Place _____

Comments _____

_____

Time _____ Event _____

Place _____

Comments _____

_____

Time _____ Event _____

Place _____

Comments _____

_____

Time _____ Event _____

Place _____

Comments _____

_____

Reception Traditions

The First Dance. The traditional order of partners for the first dance is:

1. You and your groom alone.
2. Your father cuts in to dance with you while the groom dances with your mother.
3. The groom's father cuts in to dance with you and the groom dances with his mother.
4. The best man dances with you and the groom dances with the honor attendant.
5. The whole wedding party joins you on the dance floor.
6. All the guests join you.

Ask your band leader or master of ceremonies to announce the dance so that everyone will clear the floor. Dispense with tradition if your parents are divorced and the order of partners would be awkward. You and your groom can take a spin and then ask your guests to join in.

The Toasts. Traditionally, the best man makes the first toast to the couple, then the groom toasts the bride and her family, and the bride toasts the groom and *his* family. Try to schedule the toasting so that it doesn't interfere with the meal or any of the other events you have planned.

Cutting the Cake. Traditionally, the bride holds the knife (a beribboned silver cake knife) to cut the first slice of the cake, and the groom puts his hand over hers. They feed each other from that slice, then distribute pieces to their new families. Usually, the catering staff or a host or hostess then steps in to cut the rest, having removed the top tier to be frozen for use on the couple's first anniversary. You may provide special napkins or boxes (sometimes printed with your names and the date of the wedding) so that your guests can take a slice home. (Young girls traditionally sleep on these wedding napkins and dream of their husbands-to-be.)

The Bouquet and Garter Toss. These are traditionally the last events of a reception, signs that the festivities are winding down and the bride and groom are close to making their getaway. All the single bridesmaids and female guests gather for a chance to catch the bridal bouquet that will mean she's the next to walk down the aisle. If you're reluctant to give up your bouquet, you can have a smaller one made to throw instead or a pull-out section built in to the arrangement.

Then the single men gather for the garter toss. Make sure to wear the garter in an easily accessible place (close to your knee), so your husband doesn't have to grope for it. If you'd rather not reveal your legs, wear a wrist garter!

Believe it or not, the most challenging aspects of planning your wedding are behind you. The big picture is drawn. The next chapters—food, photography, flowers and decorations, and invitations—are the details of that special wedding picture that is uniquely yours.

Romantic morsels to feed each other as your first nourishment as husband and wife.
Cake art from Polly's Cakes in Portland, Oregon.

Seven

FOOD FOR OUR WEDDING

PLANNING YOUR MENU

OTHING DOES MORE for a celebration than food! This is especially true in the communities of the African Diaspora, where cooking connotes culture. While your food might be prepared by family and church members or by a caterer or be included in an overall package deal for your wedding festivities, you still want it to reflect your tastes. This chapter is designed to help you make your wedding meal the most memorable of your life. It is also intended to help you consider the other occasions during your wedding preparations and following the wedding where you may want to serve food.

As you plan the food with family and friends who will cook for you or interview caterers and visit sites that include food in a package deal, consider whether or not they fit into your wedding vision. Are they able to provide the type of food you enjoy and that your family traditionally serves? Be sure, if you are selecting a caterer, to compare the costs for service for different times of the day and various menus, making sure to stay within your budget.

The reception is, of course, the biggest food event of your nuptial celebrations. Use the work sheet below to plan the food that suits your taste, whether it be barbecue or smoked tofu.

❧ Reception Menu List

Budget $_____

Number of guests _____

Style   Buffet ❑   Sit-down ❑   Cocktails/Hors d'oeuvres ❑   Cake and Punch ❑

MENU A	MENU B	MENU C
Style_____	Style_____	Style_____
Kind of service_____	Kind of service_____	Kind of service_____
Caterer_____	Caterer_____	Caterer_____
Cost $_____	Cost $_____	Cost $_____

Food

Appetizers _____   _____   _____

_____   _____   _____

_____   _____   _____

Main dishes _____   _____   _____

_____   _____   _____

_____   _____   _____

Side dishes _____   _____   _____

_____   _____   _____

_____   _____   _____

Breads _____   _____   _____

_____   _____   _____

_____   _____   _____

Salads _____   _____   _____

_____   _____   _____

_____   _____   _____

Desserts _____   _____   _____

_____   _____   _____

_____   _____   _____

Beverages

Alcoholic
_____   _____   _____

_____   _____   _____

_____   _____   _____

Nonalcoholic
_____   _____   _____

_____   _____   _____

_____   _____   _____

Coffee, tea
_____   _____   _____

_____   _____   _____

_____   _____   _____

Considerations for Choosing Wedding Beverages

There are only three things to consider when deciding what to serve to quench the thirst at your reception: your food, guests, and values. Others would tell you to consider budget, but we believe if you satisfy these three considerations, you can find libation at a wide range of prices, and there will be something within your budget.

Start with the *values*—yours and those of your guests. If alcoholic beverages would cause concern, you might decide to rule out reception cocktails and wine with dinner. Choose an elegant sparkling cider or a fizzy, flavored mineral water. Check out your local health food store for a surprisingly wide variety of sophisticated beverages that are bottled like wine and serve up splendidly.

Then consider your *guests*. Be honest. Will your husband-to-be's frat brothers turn your reception into a brawl? Will your aunts and uncles get in their cups and make it a bluesy, rather than a joyful, event? Imagine your guests driving home. If you have a calm, peaceful feeling, then perhaps alcohol can add a pleasant buzz to your reception. If the thought leaves you uneasy, consider an alcohol-free celebration or perhaps a simple champagne toast.

Good *food* has many accompaniments. If your values and guests give you the green light for wine, follow the simple light with light and dark with dark rule. That is, white wines with fish, chicken, turkey, and pale meats like pork (chitterlings and Chardonnay, yum!) and red wines with beef, barbecue, duck, and other heavier fare, such as pasta with tomato sauces.

MORNING-AFTER BRUNCH

It is becoming more and more common for couples to provide food for family and guests from out of town the morning after the wedding. Here is a work sheet if you would like to show this kindness to your guests. It's a perfect opportunity for you to spend some extra time with such special loved ones and show your appreciation for the extra effort they made to be with you on your special day.

❧ *Morning-After Brunch Menu Work Sheet*

Budget $_____

Number of guests _____

Style   Buffet ❏   Sit-down ❏

Kind of service _____

Caterer _____

Cost $ _____

Food

Main dishes _____

_____

_____

_____

Side dishes _____

_____

_____

_____

Breads _____

_____

_____

_____

Salads _____

_____

_____

_____

Desserts_____

_____

_____

_____

Beverages

Alcoholic _____

_____

_____

Nonalcoholic _____

_____

_____

Coffee, tea _____

_____

_____

The rehearsal dinner is another occasion for which you may want to consider serving food. Your wedding party includes your most intimate family and friends. Sharing a meal together is a great way to let his and your friends bond and for you all to cherish the special moments of laughter, confusion, and depth of feeling this shadow wedding will inevitably create.

❧ *Rehearsal Dinner Work Sheet*

Budget $_____

Number of guests _____

Style   Buffet ❑   Sit-down ❑   Cocktails/Hors d'oeuvres ❑   Cake and punch ❑

MENU A	MENU B	MENU C
Style_____	Style_____	Style_____
Kind of service _____	Kind of service _____	Kind of service _____
Caterer_____	Caterer_____	Caterer_____
Cost $_____	Cost $_____	Cost $_____

Food

Hors d'oeuvres_____	_____	_____
_____	_____	_____
_____	_____	_____

Appetizers _____ _____ _____

_____ _____ _____

_____ _____ _____

Main dishes _____ _____ _____

_____ _____ _____

_____ _____ _____

Side dishes _____ _____ _____

_____ _____ _____

_____ _____ _____

Breads _____ _____ _____

_____ _____ _____

_____ _____ _____

Salads _____ _____ _____

_____ _____ _____

_____ _____ _____

Desserts _____ _____ _____

_____ _____ _____

_____ _____ _____

Beverages

Alcoholic
_____ _____ _____

_____ _____ _____

_____ _____ _____

Nonalcoholic
_____ _____ _____

_____ _____ _____

_____ _____ _____

Coffee, tea
_____ _____ _____

_____ _____ _____

_____ _____ _____

CATERING CONTRACT

Your caterer will probably have a preprinted contract, but just in case, here is a sample you may wish to use. Be sure the caterer's contract includes all of the items listed here, especially the overtime charges and details of the staff provided.

❧ *Catering Contract Checklist*

Event _____ Date _____

Style _____

Starting time _____ Ending time _____

Number of guests _____

Caterer _____

Staff provided (specify type) _____

Staff provided (specify type) _____

Contact _____

Address _____

Phone _____ Fax _____

Food

Hors d'oeuvres _____

_____

_____

_____

_____

Appetizers _____

_____

_____

Main dishes

_____

_____

_____

_____

Side dishes

_____

_____

_____

_____

Breads

_____

_____

_____

_____

Salads

_____

_____

_____

_____

_____

Desserts

_____

_____

_____

_____

_____

Wedding Cake

Bride's cake   _____

Groom's cake   _____

Beverages

Alcoholic   _____

_____

_____

Nonalcoholic _____

_____

_____

Coffee, tea _____

_____

_____

Decorations_____

Other services _____

Equipment _____

_____

Cost $_____ (per person)   Gratuities_____%   Sales Tax_____%

Overtime fee $ _____(per hour)   Total $_____

Terms of payment: Deposit due $_____   Date due_____

Final payment $_____   Date due _____

Cancellation policy _____

IF FOOD'S A FAMILY-AND-FRIENDS AFFAIR

No one says you must have a caterer, and in the Black community, many wedding feasts are still lovingly prepared the old-fashioned way—by friends and family. Many of those who love you will want to show their love the best way they know how—by bringing their best dish or one they know you especially enjoy.

But, as nuptial gatherings have increased in size, you'll want to use all the planning tools modern life provides to be sure that there is plenty of food for all, that you have the serving conditions needed for the dishes contributed, and that the menu is balanced. (You don't want fifteen pots of collards and nothing else!) Here are work sheets to help you organize the food preparation.

❧ Cooks for Our Wedding List

NAME	PHONE	NAME OF DISH

❧ Menu for Our Wedding

APPETIZERS

1. _____
2. _____
3. _____
4. _____
5. _____

WHO'S PREPARING

_____
_____
_____
_____
_____

MEATS/FISH/MAIN DISHES

1. _____
2. _____
3. _____
4. _____
5. _____

WHO'S PREPARING

_____
_____
_____
_____
_____

SIDE DISHES

1. _____
2. _____
3. _____
4. _____
5. _____
6. _____
7. _____

WHO'S PREPARING

_____
_____
_____
_____
_____
_____
_____

8. _____   _____

9. _____   _____

10. _____   _____

BREADS

WHO'S PREPARING

1. _____   _____

2. _____   _____

3. _____   _____

4. _____   _____

5. _____   _____

SALADS

WHO'S PREPARING

1. _____   _____

2. _____   _____

3. _____   _____

4. _____   _____

5. _____   _____

DESSERTS

WHO'S PREPARING

1. _____   _____

2. _____   _____

3. _____   _____

4. _____   _____

5. _____   _____

WEDDING CAKE	**WHO'S PREPARING**
1._____	_____
2._____	_____

$ _____for ingredients

$ _____for rental of baking/assembly items

Name of recipe to be used _____

A few words about homemade wedding cakes: First, don't fear. Making wedding cakes at home is a strong tradition in communities of the Diaspora across the United States and the Caribbean. But do make sure the friend or family member who prepares your cake is experienced. Discreetly ask others for whom she has prepared a wedding cake. Then be sure to ask her to give you a taste test of the recipe you are asking her to prepare for you. The rehearsal dinner (provided it is not the night before the wedding!) might be a good place for her to test a mini version of the cake.

Wedding cakes, when successful, are among the most remembered elements of Black weddings. Likely this is because baking at home is such a strong part of our culinary tradition. In anticipation that you'll want to recreate (or have recreated) your wedding cake, record the recipe here.

OUR WEDDING CAKE RECIPE

Name _____

Provided by _____

Interesting facts/tradition about this recipe _____

_____

_____

_____

Ingredients

_____

_____

_____

_____

_____

_____

_____

_____

_____

_____

_____

_____

_____

_____

_____

_____

_____

_____

_____

_____

Equipment needed

_____

_____

_____

_____

_____

_____

_____

_____

_____

_____

Oven Settings_____

_____

Batter Preparation Steps

1. _____

2. _____

3. _____

4. _____

5. _____

6. _____

7. _____

8. _____

9. _____

10. _____

11. _____

12. _____

13. _____

14. _____

15. _____

16. _____

17. _____

18. _____

19. _____

20. _____

Icing Preparation Steps

1. _____

2. _____

3. _____

4. _____

5. _____

Baking Instructions_____

_____

_____

_____

_____

_____

Cooling Instructions_____

_____

_____

_____

Assembly Instructions _____

_____

_____

_____

These chocolate boxes, with real removable chocolate lids from Polly's Cakes, make great favors for your guests or serve as lovely decorations on the wedding cake table.

IF OTHERS ARE COOKING YOUR SELECTED RECIPES

It's becoming more and more popular for friends and family to prepare food for weddings from menus of the couple's choice. (But be sure to get approval at your site. Many banquet halls require licensed food handlers for all events.) There are several good books devoted solely to this subject, which indicate the need for tight organization and planning. Use the work sheets above, but additionally be sure to provide all the recipes *in writing*. Use the following blank pages, in which you may tape photocopies of the recipes and note who is preparing them. Plan occasions to test the recipes before the wedding. Also, be sensitive to the cost of ingredients (and your savings by not hiring a caterer!) and offer to buy the ingredients.

As you plan for a homemade reception, remember, the *preparation* of the food is part of the festivities and a show of love by those who cook for your wedding. Don't forget to send each one a formal Thank You note!

Paste photocopies of your recipes here.

Paste photocopies of your recipes here.

Paste photocopies of your recipes here.

❧ *Recipes Work Sheet*

To be prepared by _____

$ _____provided for ingredients

_____date tested

To be brought to _____   Time _____

Thank You note sent _____

To be prepared by _____

$ _____provided for ingredients

_____date tested

To be brought to _____   Time _____

Thank You note sent _____

To be prepared by _____

$ _____provided for ingredients

_____date tested

To be brought to _____   Time _____

Thank You note sent _____

The right photography will capture not only the day's events but its mood and the
poignant moments memories are made of.

PLANNING A PICTURE-PERFECT

WEDDING ALBUM

OUR BIG DAY HAPPENS only once, but the photos will help you relive it for years to come and can even become cherished family heirloom items. That's why we recommend you choose a photographer carefully. Seek recommendations from relatives and friends who used professional photographers for their wedding and were satisfied with their work. Ask to see his or her actual portfolio of wedding work. Pay attention to the skin tones in the portfolio shots to be sure the photographer understands how to light and photograph people of color. Because people of the Diaspora come in every color, your photographer needs to know how to handle lighting for a wide range of complexions. If you want lots of family shots and special group shots, look for examples in your photographer's portfolio.

Hire a photographer who uses a medium-format camera, not a 35mm. The negatives from the medium format are larger than the negatives from a 35mm, giving better resolution and print clarity. His or her fee and that of any assistants will depend on the number of hours they are contracted to shoot, as well as the equipment setup, lighting, and handling of the film. Remember, you will need photos not only on the wedding day but for newspaper announcements, as well.

Here are some specific questions to ask:

- What is his or her training and experience in wedding photography?
- May we have three client references, especially clients of color? (Contact them.)
- Has the photographer shot at the site of your ceremony and reception before? (It can be useful to have someone who is already familiar with the lighting requirements at a particular location.)
- Will the photographer have an assistant?
- How are his or her rates based? (Some charge a flat fee for a certain number of hours, then charge overtime. Get the specifics of what's included in the cost.)
- Does he or she shoot more than the standard album quantity? (Standard usually means couple, wedding party, ceremony, and reception shots.)
- How many photos will you have to choose from?
- For how long are you allowed to keep the negatives?
- Will the wedding album have a logical pictorial sequence?
- Does he or she shoot candid, spontaneous shots at no extra cost?
- What lighting methods are available? (Again, the photographer needs to know how to make all skin tones look natural.)

Photographer Interview Work Sheet

Photographer Possibility #1 _____

Address_____ City _____ State _____ Zip code _____

Phone_____ Fax _____

Number of assistants_____ Available on our date_____

Services to be performed _____

Budget $_____ Cost $_____

References _____

_____

Comments _____

_____

Photographer Possibility #2 _____

Address_____ City _____ State _____ Zip code _____

Phone_____ Fax _____

Number of assistants_____ Available on our date_____

Services to be performed _____

Budget $_____ Cost $_____

References _____

_____

Comments _____

_____

Photographer Possibility #3 _____

Address_____ City _____ State _____ Zip code _____

Phone_____ Fax _____

Number of assistants_____ Available on our date_____

Services to be performed _____

Budget $_____ Cost $_____

References _____

_____

Comments _____

_____

Once you've picked the photographer, get a contract. The photographer will likely have his or her own contract form, but be sure all the terms listed on our checklist are agreed upon in advance and in writing. If you're using a studio, you will want the names of the photographers assigned to cover your wedding noted in your contract. Also specify in the contract the photographer's attire, which must blend in with the wedding guests to be as unnoticeable as possible.

❧ Contract Checklist

Photographer _____

Address _____ City _____ State _____ Zip code _____

Phone _____ Fax _____

Number of assistants _____

Engagement photograph _____

Date and time _____

Proofs due _____

Cost $ _____

Bridal portrait _____

Date and time _____

Proofs due _____

Cost $ _____

Equipment _____

No. of cameras _____

Description _____

Number of rolls of color film _____

Number of rolls of black & white film _____

Number of frames and style _____

Number of proofs _____

Color _____

Black & white_____

Number of prints_____

Albums

    Bride and bridegroom _____

    Parents of the bride _____

    Parents of the bridegroom _____

Description of package _____

Proofs due _____ Album delivery date _____

Overtime fee _____

Date of deposit _____ Amount of deposit $ _____

Balance due $ _____ Total cost $ _____

One of the biggest regrets we hear after weddings is that the photographer did not get that special moment when . . . Make sure your wedding album includes everything you want to remember by providing your camera person with a schedule of

shots of particular events that are special to you, i.e., your Yoruba herb tasting ceremony, candle lighting, jumping the broom, etc., and a photo list of family members and friends you want to show celebrating your wedding. Attach this list to the photographer's contract. And don't forget to keep a copy of this list, too!

The right photographer will make the entire bridal party look their best

❧ *Wedding Photographs Work Sheet*

Photographer _____

Date of event _____

Locations and times of arrival _____

    Before the ceremony _____ _____

    Ceremony site _____ _____

    Park site _____ _____

    Reception site _____ _____

Checklist of Special Shots

- ❑ View of the church
- ❑ Bride's mother adjusting the veil
- ❑ Bridegroom and best man looking at their watches
- ❑ The bridal procession
- ❑ The bride and groom at the altar
- ❑ Pouring of the libation
- ❑ Bitter herb tasting
- ❑ The exchange of rings
- ❑ Exchange of kola nuts
- ❑ The kiss
- ❑ The signing of the marriage certificate
- ❑ You and your groom as you leave the church
- ❑ You and your groom with your parents and his
- ❑ You and your groom with the whole wedding party
- ❑ The bridesmaids alone
- ❑ The groomsmen alone
- ❑ Toasts at the reception
- ❑ The first dance
- ❑ Cutting the cake
- ❑ Throwing the bouquet
- ❑ Your getaway as you leave for your honeymoon
- ❑ Hands together with rings
- ❑ Broom jumping
- ❑ Group shot of family and friends who have traveled a long distance
- ❑ Other _____

_____

_____

_____

Avideotaped recording of your ceremony will also bring back fond memories of your Big Day, and more and more couples are choosing this option along with still photos. You must choose a videographer carefully. Often, the best way to find a video person is through your photographer. When interviewing for the video work, ask if they do their own editing and dubbing and if so, if they have up-to-date machines. Ask to see a video of their most recent wedding. Note their editing techniques. Does it seem to run smoothly, going from one segment of the event to the next? Is it a sharp steady picture? Is it framed nicely? Is the sound clear? Is it telling the wedding day story, or does it seem to be out of sequence?

Perhaps you'd like a family member or friend to shoot videos of you during your pre-wedding planning activities—shopping for your gown, the groom selecting the tuxedos for himself and the groomsmen, or you two selecting your rings. Ask the videographer if he or she can edit these into the tape to tell the entire story of your pre-planning as well as your wedding day.

Use the work sheets below to interview and make a contract with your videographer.

❧ *Videography Work Sheet*

Videographer _____

Address _____

City _____ State_____ Zip code_____

Phone_____ Fax _____

Number of assistants_____

Services _____

Special effects_____

_____

Number of video cameras_____

Number of microphones

    Boom _____

    Wired_____

    Wireless_____

Cost $ _____

References _____

_____

Comments_____

_____

Videographer _____

Address _____

City _____ State_____ Zip code_____

Phone_____ Fax _____

Number of assistants_____

Services _____

Special effects_____

_____

Number of video cameras_____

Number of microphones

    Boom _____

Wired _____

Wireless _____

Cost $ _____

References _____

_____

Comments _____

_____

Videographer _____

Address _____

City _____ State _____ Zip code _____

Phone _____ Fax _____

Number of assistants _____

Services _____

Special effects _____

_____

Number of video cameras _____

Number of microphones

Boom _____

Wired _____

Wireless _____

Cost $ _____

References _____

_____

Comments_____

_____

❧ *Videography Contract Checklist*

Videographer _____

Address _____

City _____ State_____ Zip code_____

Phone_____ Fax _____

Assistants_____

_____

Date of event_____

Location and time of arrival

    Before the ceremony _____ _____

    Ceremony site_____ _____

    Park site_____ _____

    Reception site _____ _____

Cost per hour $_____ Overtime fee per hour $_____

Number of video cameras_____ Number of tapes_____

In-camera editing: yes ❑ no ❑   Postediting: yes ❑ no ❑

Description of package _____

_____

Special effects_____

_____

Date of deposit _____   Amount $_____

Balance due date_____   Amount $_____

Delivery date _____

Total cost $ _____

Once you have contracts with the photographer and videographer, give each the name and phone number of the other, and ask them to coordinate their activities.

By the time you have completed this planning section, you'll likely have a deck of photographs, as many photographers won't be able to resist snapping a few shots of you as you interview them. Here's a place to keep those in-process shots for the days ahead when you'll look back in wonder. *But* don't paste them in until you've completed the book. They'll make your planner lumpy, and writing on them will be a bigger challenge than planning your wedding!

Paste your favorite photos here.

Paste your favorite photos here.

Something old as Africa, something new, something floral, that expresses you!

Nine

ARRANGING YOUR FLOWERS

—AND MORE

OU'VE GOTTEN ALL the really hard work off to a good start:

the clothes, the place, the officiant, the bridal party, the

food, and the recording of the special day in pictures. It's

all creative and it's all fun, but no other aspect of wedding planning is as special as choos-

ing flowers and other decorations for your wedding celebrations.

As people of the African Diaspora, we have a inherited a strong connection to the Earth, and making floral selections for your wedding is an opportunity to celebrate that heritage.

Most couples underbudget for flowers. Flowers are what the bride carries with her down the aisle, right? The next work sheet tells you the answer. Everyone in the wedding party as well as all the women close to the two of you—mothers, grandmothers, godmothers (this includes other-mothers, too!), and those special sister-friends who will serve as hostesses—will appreciate wearing flowers. And you'll want flowers to bring their blessing of beauty and fragrance to the ceremony and reception sites and banquet tables.

Don't forget flowers—perhaps wild ones—for those special sister-friends who'll keep life spicy even after you're married.

As you fit flowers into your wedding vision, think flowers-plus. Consider using dried or silk flowers as well as fresh, and grains and other foliage to represent the bounties of the harvest. Flowers tied with lace, flowers wrapped in African fabric, flowers dotted with beads, flowers in baskets, flowers woven into sprays or wreaths, flowers accompanied by a meaningful keepsake favor, or any of a thousand other ways flowers partner with lovely objects. Which will be the combination that will achieve your wedding vision?

And don't limit yourself to flowers. Balloons are an increasingly popular addition to wedding celebrations—colorfully released at the end of the ceremony or formed into archways and columns at the reception. Or dazzle your guests with dramatic ice sculptures in shapes reflecting the theme of your wedding. Carefully consider the visual impression you want your ceremony and reception sites to make as well as the clothing choices you have made. Then use the following work sheet to create the setting of your dreams.

🕊️ *Flowers and Decorations Work Sheet*

	QUANTITY	DESCRIPTION	COST/ITEM	TOTAL COST

Bridal Bouquets

	QUANTITY	DESCRIPTION	COST/ITEM	TOTAL COST
Bride				
Maid/matron of honor				
Bridesmaid(s)				
Flower girl(s)				
Junior bridesmaids(s)				
Ring bearer's pillow				

Boutonnieres

	QUANTITY	DESCRIPTION	COST/ITEM	TOTAL COST
Bridegroom				
Best man				
Groomsmen				
Ushers				
Junior ushers				
Ring bearer				
Train bearers				
Pages				
Father of the bride				
Father of the groom				

	QUANTITY	DESCRIPTION	COST/ITEM	TOTAL COST
Grandfather of the bride				
Grandfather of the groom				
Godfather of the bride				
Godfather of the groom				
Host(s)				

Corsages

Mother of the bride				
Mother of the groom				
Grandmother of the bride				
Grandmother of the groom				
Godmother of the bride				
Godmother of the groom				
Hostesses				

Ceremony Site

Church altar				
Pew bows				
Aisle carpet/runner				

	QUANTITY	DESCRIPTION	COST/ITEM	TOTAL COST

Reception Site

	QUANTITY	DESCRIPTION	COST/ITEM	TOTAL COST
Entryway/lobby	_____	_____	_____	_____
Food tables/ serving stations	_____	_____	_____	_____
Bar	_____	_____	_____	_____
Head table	_____	_____	_____	_____
Guests' tables	_____	_____	_____	_____
Other	_____	_____	_____	_____

You may choose to comb the wholesale flower district or shops of your city and find those blooms that perfectly express your wedding vision, or, like most couples, you may decide to use the expertise of a florist.

Before selecting a florist, the date, places, and times of your wedding celebrations and the style of your gown and the bridesmaids' dresses must be established. If you have not finished making those decisions, hold off on deciding on a florist. You may still interview them, however. Be sure to hire a professional florist who has a good reputation, has been established for some time, and can show you samples to assure you that she can produce the style you envision. This is especially true if you are seeking Afrocentric-style bouquets and arrangements.

Bring swatches of your gown and attendants' dresses to the interview with the florist and bring Polaroids of the ceremony and reception sites. To determine the extent of the florist's artistry, ask for photos of other weddings she has done and get several references. Be sure to see samples of the full range of her talents, from corsages to centerpieces. Here are a few questions you will want to ask:

- Are you familiar with my wedding sites?
- What flowers will be in season at the time of my wedding?
- How can we ensure that we get the flowers we want?
- Do you provide a freshness guarantee?
- Do you decorate and, if so, what can you do to decorate the sites within my budget?
- Will you be there on the day of the wedding?
- Do you charge delivery and setup fees?

Adapt these questions to your interviews with other decorators, such as balloon artists and ice sculptors. Have they worked at your sites before? What special equipment do they need?

Use the following work sheets to compare costs and services.

Styles for Your Bouquet

Arm Bouquet—Composed of long-stemmed flowers that are hand-tied or French-braided with ribbon and carried cradled in the arm.

Biedermeier—A small, compact bouquet with rings of flowers, one inside the other, each ring consisting of a different flower and often of a different color.

Boa—A garland of flowers and greens wired together so that it can be worn draped around the shoulders or beauty-queen style, diagonally across the bodice.

Cascade—An arrangement of flowers and greens that cascades down from the holder

Composite—New flowers are created by gluing or wiring different petals and blossoms together, often one inside the other. For instance, a glamelia consists of multiple gladiola blossoms stuffed inside each other to give the appearance of a camellia.

Nosegay—A small, round arrangement, in a holder or hand-tied.

Pomander—Flowers are inserted into a globe-shaped oasis to achieve a ball-shaped bouquet that can be carried hanging from a ribbon.

Tussie-Mussie—A hand-tied bouquet of flowers (each chosen for its symbolic meaning) whose stems have been cut to a manageable length and trimmed with a ribbon or inserted into a silver cone-shaped holder. Popular in Victorian times.

Wired—Each flower is wired along the length of its stem so that it can be sculpted into an overall design.

❧ *Florist/Decorator Work Sheet*

Florist/Decorator #1

Company name _____

Contact person _____

Address _____

City _____ State_____ Zip code_____

Phone_____ Fax _____

Services _____

_____

Cost $ _____

References _____

_____

Comments _____

_____

Florist/Decorator #2

Company name _____

Contact person _____

Address _____

City _____ State_____ Zip code_____

Phone_____ Fax _____

Services _____

_____

Cost $ _____

References _____

_____

Comments _____

_____

Florist / Decorator #3

Company name _____

Contact person _____

Address _____

City _____ State_____ Zip code_____

Phone_____ Fax _____

Services _____

_____

Cost $ _____

References _____

_____

Comments _____

_____

Traditional Wedding Flowers

APPLE BLOSSOMS
for good fortune

BLUE VIOLETS
for faithfulness

GARDENIAS
for joy

LILACS
for first love

LILIES
for purity and innocence

LILY OF THE VALLEY
for return of happiness

ORANGE BLOSSOMS
for purity and fertility
(an orange tree blossoms and bears fruit at the same time)

ORCHIDS
for passion

ROSES
for romance

Once you have the information you need to provide to the florist or decorator and have interviewed and checked references for several, you are ready to make a decision. As with all your vendors, a contract is a must. Most florists and other decorators will have their own preprinted contract, but use the one below if she doesn't. In using the vendor's own contract, be sure it includes all the items on our work sheet or attach our work sheet to it. Since you may be having flowers or other decorations delivered to your home or locations other than your cermony and reception sites, we've provided three delivery options.

❧ Florist/Decorator Contract

Company name _____

Contact person _____

Address _____

City _____ State_____ Zip code_____

Phone_____ Fax _____

Order (see attached list) _____

Date of delivery_____

Time of delivery #1 _____

Location of delivery #1 _____

Time of delivery #2 _____

Location of delivery #2 _____

Time of delivery #3 _____

Location of delivery #3 _____

Date of deposit _____

Special services at ceremony site _____

Special services at reception site _____

Amount of deposit $_____

Balance due $ _____

Total cost $ _____

This collage of invitations is only the beginning of the wide range of expressions available for your wedding stationery items. *Afrocentric invitation courtesy of Invitations by Dawn® mail order catalog.*

Ten

PLANNING AND SENDING

YOUR INVITATIONS

VERYONE KNOWS YOU'RE getting married, but your wedding invitation tells your guests the who and when and where and much more. The lining of the envelope, the style of the lettering, the color of the ink, the weight of the paper—every detail reflects your total vision for your Big Day. Your invitation can say it loud or say it softly, can signal formal or informal, can echo the voices of your ancestors or speak in your own heartfelt words.

Now that you've made your guest list and reserved your ceremony and reception sites, you have all the information you need to prepare your invitation. If you've hired a wedding consultant, she probably has catalogues from mail-order invitation houses that you can page through for ideas about typeface, paper, color, and decorative elements. Or you can consult your *Yellow Pages* under "Invitations and Announcements" for local stationers, department stores, and printers who can show you samples.

The three basic printing techniques for invitations are:

- Engraving, the most traditional and expensive method, which uses a metal die to cut the letters into the paper so they are raised on the front of the invitation
- Thermography, less expensive than engraving, which *applies* the letters to the surface so that they feel raised
- Offset printing, the least expensive method, which just transfers ink to the surface of the paper

Black is the traditional choice for the color of ink and a white or ivory folded sheet of fine, heavy weight paper. You may want to choose an ink or paper coordinated with your color scheme or add an African-patterned border with a matching foil lining in your envelope or reproduce a cherished photograph or piece of artwork as part of your design. Explore all the different options until you find the right combination of elements for your wedding. Keep a record of your ideas and their estimated costs in the Invitation Style Work Sheet that follows.

❧ *Invitation Style Work Sheet*

Invitation budget _____

Estimated quantity _____

Choice #1

ELEMENTS	ESTIMATED COST
Size (____ x ____)	_____
Printing techniques:	
Engraving	_____
Thermography	_____
Offset	_____
Paper_____	_____
Foil_____	_____
Borders_____	_____
Graphics _____	_____
Type style _____	_____
Folds _____	_____
Other special elements_____	_____
Total	$ _____

Choice #2

ELEMENTS	ESTIMATED COST
Size (____ x ____)	_____
Printing techniques:	_____
Engraving	_____
Thermography	_____
Offset	_____
Paper_____	_____
Foil _____	_____
Borders_____	_____
Graphics _____	_____
Type style _____	_____
Folds _____	_____
Other special elements_____	_____
Total	$ _____

Choice #3

ELEMENTS	ESTIMATED COST
Size (____ x ____)	_____
Printing techniques:	_____
Engraving	_____
Thermography	_____
Offset	_____

	ELEMENTS	ESTIMATED COST
Paper	_____	_____
Foil	_____	_____
Borders	_____	_____
Graphics	_____	_____
Type style	_____	_____
Folds	_____	_____
Other special elements	_____	_____
	Total	$ _____

WORDING

Before you think about the wording that will make your invitation special, you want to be sure to include all the information your guests will need to get to the ceremony site on time and appropriately dressed. Carefully fill in the Wording Checklist here and use it to double-check your final copy. Spell out all the names and numbers (except zip codes and street numbers longer than two digits).

❧ *Wording Checklist*

Names of those issuing the invitation _____

_____

The date and time of day _____

The place _____

_____

The attire expected _____

Request for response and address or telephone number _____

_____

Sample Traditional
Invitation Wording

Traditionally, the bride's parents issue the invitation:

Mr. and Mrs. Henry Palmer
request the honour of your presence
at the marriage of their daughter
Nichole
to
Gregory Driver
on Saturday, the third of October
Nineteen hundred and ninety-nine
at four o'clock in the afternoon
Central Baptist Church
1234 Any Street
Anytown, Anystate
and afterward in
the Church Hall

R.S.V.P.
Street address
City, State zip code

Note that in this case the reception is being held at the same location as the ceremony, and all the guests are invited.

If you are asking only certain guests to the reception, you'd use a separate reception card and omit the R.S.V.P. from the invitation to the ceremony.

Mr. and Mrs. Henry Palmer
request the pleasure of your company
at the reception
immediately following the ceremony
at their home
Thirty-Three Hawthorne Street

R.S.V.P.

Note that the invitation now requests "the pleasure of your company" because the occasion is now social rather than sacred.

If your parents are no longer together but still want to issue a joint invitation:

Olivia Patterson Palmer
(your mother's first, maiden, and married names—or her new married name if she has remarried)
and
Henry Palmer
request the honour of your presence
at the marriage of their daughter
Nichole
to
Gregory Driver . . .

If one of your parents is no longer living, the surviving parent issues the invitation in his or her own name:

Mrs. Henry Palmer
requests the honour of your presence
at the marriage of her daughter
Nichole
to
Gregory Driver . . .

If both sets of parents issue the invitation, as they might for an Afrocentric ceremony:

Mr. and Mrs. Henry Palmer
request the honour of your presence
at the marriage of their daughter
Nichole
to
Gregory Driver
son of Mr. and Mrs. George Driver . . .

or

Mr. and Mrs. Henry Palmer
and
Mr. and Mrs. George Driver
request the honour of your presence
at the marriage of their children
Nichole
and Gregory

A version acknowledging our African heritage might be:

Mr. and Mrs. Henry Palmer
request the honour of your presence
in a traditional unity ceremony
joining their daughter
Nichole
to
Gregory Driver
son of Mr. and Mrs. George Driver . . .

Of course the words of your invitation convey more than time and place and degree of formality. You may want to incorporate poetry or Bible verses that have special meaning for you, or you may want to choose non-traditional wording that suggests the spiritual or cultural context of your ceremony. Many invitation houses offer a selection of contemporary alternatives, including verses and Afrocentric wordings that emphasize our ancestry and the importance of family traditions. Or perhaps you'd like to use the space below to compose your invitation in your own words. (Twelve lines are standard for an invitation. If your invitation is longer, check with your dealer about additional charges.)

❧ Invitation Wording

_____

_____

_____

_____

_____

_____

_____

_____

_____

_____

_____

_____

Your invitation (and its envelope) is probably not the only piece of wedding stationery you'll need. Depending on the style and formality of your ceremony, you may want to order the following:

- Protective tissue, to keep the ink from smudging on an engraved invitation, but may be added as a decorative element even if you're using another printing technique; sometimes supplied at no cost
- An inner envelope as well as an outer one
- A separate reception card
- Response card
- "Within the ribbons" cards for guests who will have reserved seating
- Maps to help guests find your ceremony or reception site
- Parking or transportation cards if you make special arrangements
- At-home cards to announce your married name and address.

Besides these additional enclosures for your invitation, you can also order printed favors or mementos for your reception, wedding announcements to send to those you can't invite, acknowledgment cards for gifts received, Thank You notes, and personal stationery. Assess your needs and keep track of quantities and costs with the following work sheet.

❧ *Other Elements and Enclosures List*

STYLE/DESCRIPTION NO.	QUANTITY	COST
Invitation _____	_____	$ _____
Protective tissue _____	_____	$ _____
Outer envelopes _____	_____	$ _____
Inner envelopes _____	_____	$ _____
Reception cards _____	_____	$ _____
Response cards _____	_____	$ _____
"Within the ribbons" cards_____	_____	$ _____
Maps _____	_____	$ _____
At-home cards_____	_____	$ _____
Wedding programs _____	_____	$ _____
Wedding announcements _____	_____	$ _____
Acknowledgment of gifts received ____	_____	$ _____
Thank You notes _____	_____	$ _____
Personal stationery _____	_____	$ _____
Favors and mementos _____	_____	$ _____
Parking cards _____	_____	$ _____
Hotel accommodation cards _____	_____	$ _____
Other (specify) _____	_____	$ _____
Other (specify) _____	_____	$ _____
Total cost		$ _____

O nce you've decided on the style and wording of your invitations, the enclosures, personal stationery, and other printed pieces, you're ready to place your order (ideally three to six months before the ceremony). Order at least 50 extra sets and 100 extra envelopes to have on hand in case of mistakes in addressing or late additions to your guest list. Use the Ordering Checklist here to make sure you don't overlook anything and to keep track of payments and delivery dates.

❧ Invitation Order Work Sheet

Budget $_____

Dealer name and address _____

_____

_____

Date ordered_____

ITEM	ITEM NUMBER	QUANTITY	PRICE EACH	TOTAL PRICE
Invitation	_____	_____	$_____	$_____
Protective tissue	_____	_____	$_____	$_____
Outer envelopes	_____	_____	$_____	$_____
Inner envelopes	_____	_____	$_____	$_____
Reception cards	_____	_____	$_____	$_____
Response cards	_____	_____	$_____	$_____
"Within the ribbons" cards	_____	_____	$_____	$_____

Item	Item Number	Quantity	Price Each	Total Price
Maps	_____	_____	$_____	$_____
At-home cards	_____	_____	$_____	$_____
Wedding programs	_____	_____	$_____	$_____
Wedding announcements	_____	_____	$_____	$_____
Acknowledgment of gifts received	_____	_____	$_____	$_____
Thank You notes	_____	_____	$_____	$_____
Personal stationery	_____	_____	$_____	$_____
Favors and mementos	_____	_____	$_____	$_____
Parking cards	_____	_____	$_____	$_____
Hotel accommodation cards	_____	_____	$_____	$_____
Other (specify)	_____	_____	$_____	$_____

Total cost $ _____

Date of deposit _____ Balance due date_____

Delivery date _____

Delivery address _____

City _____ State_____ Zip code_____

When your guests receive a beautifully calligraphed envelope in the mail, they'll know there's something very special inside. Hand-calligraphy is the most expensive way to address your invitations, but also the most impressive. Your wedding consultant or your invitation house can refer you to professional calligraphers or to today's new sources of computerized alternatives. You'll probably need to add an extra two or three weeks to your invitation mailing schedule for this process. Gather two or three estimates and compare them using the work sheet below. If you decide instead to do the addressing yourself (with the help of family and friends), allow at least a week.

Calligraphy Work Sheet

Calligrapher _____

Address _____

City _____ State _____ Zip code _____

Phone _____ Fax _____

Type of service _____

Quantity _____ Cost $ _____

Date of deposit _____ Balance due $ _____

Delivery date _____

Whether you hire a calligrapher or address your invitations yourself, be sure every name and address on your guest list is correct down to the last letter and number. For invitations to a family, list the children's first names alphabetically under the names of their parents. If there isn't enough room, all the boys may be addressed as "Messrs." and the girls as "Misses."

Have your local post office weigh one invitation, complete with all its elements, to gauge the cost of postage. (And pick out the prettiest stamps they have among their current issues.) Don't forget stamps for enclosed response cards!

Stuffing and Stamping

1. Put all the enclosures face-up directly on top (or inside, if it's a folded invitation).

2. Insert in the inner envelope (or the outer, if you're only using one) with the type facing the back flap.

3. If you're using an inner envelope, it should then be inserted into the outer one with the front facing the back flap so that guests see their names first when they remove it.

A small wedding (up to forty guests) or one you have only a few weeks to plan does not require a printed invitation. The mother of the bride (or the bride herself) may write short notes, fax, telephone, or even E-mail relatives and friends to invite them to the ceremony. Even if you're telephoning, take some time to consider the wording of your invitation so that your guests will know who's hosting the occasion and get a sense of your vision.

❧ Non-traditional Invitations Work Sheet

Name _____   Guest name_____

Phone_____   Fax _____

E-mail address _____

Wording_____

_____

_____

_____

_____

_____

*Your invitations have just arrived, you've checked them against your order to make sure
no mistakes were made, you've arranged to address and mail them.
Before you mail them, save one to paste here as a keepsake.*

Those who want to share in your love by giving you a gift will appreciate your making their shopping easy by registering. And you'll get gifts you choose, that you can really use.

GIVING AND RECEIVING

WITH GRACE

EFORE THE INVITATIONS have even been mailed, you probably have already received gifts. If you're like most couples of African descent, friends and family have showered you with contributions, both financial and sentimental, to make your wedding day perfect. This chapter is about making sure you receive with gratitude and acknowledge every blessing showered upon you. We know you definitely have ideas about the gifts that you would like to receive. Here we'll help you communicate graciously with those who would appreciate knowing what you actually need and would enjoy.

Registering your choices for gifts is a gift to those who give you a present. It takes the guesswork and a lot of the legwork out of the gift-giving process. So don't be shy about it! Let those closest to you know where you register, and they'll discreetly spread the word. Certainly, let folks know if they ask you specifically.

Choose department stores you like that offer a bridal registry service. Their registry consultants will be glad to show you china, silverware, crystal, linens, and other home wares and will offer suggestions about combining patterns, should you request it. Think carefully about the décor of your new home as well as the budgets of those who will be giving you gifts. Be sure to include a wide range of prices.

Try to select open patterns of china and crystal that will be available in the future, should you wish to add to what you will receive.

And be sure to consider the many alternatives to department store registries available today—from Afrocentric gift shops to specialty stores, from mortgage and honeymoon registries to donations to favorite charities (for the couple who has it all). And remember that you can register at more than one place. Mix and match all your options.

Use our work sheet to plan your choices, but keep in mind the registry services will undoubtedly have their own long, long forms for you to complete.

Dinnerware Basics

The typical place setting consists of a dinner plate, salad/dessert plate, bread and butter plate, and cup and saucer. Serving pieces may include serving platters, serving bowls, gravy boat, butter dish, and creamer and sugar bowl.

Registry consultants recommend registering for at least eight or twelve full place settings. Most manufacturers' patterns are open stock, which means that you can purchase additional pieces—or replace broken ones—individually.

Porcelain (China) is made of refined, high-quality clay that has been fired at 2800 degrees (the clay turns white during the process). The high firing temperature gives porcelain more density than earthenware, making it harder, more durable, and chip-resistant. Porcelain is a superb choice for long-lasting, fine dinnerware. It is oven-safe up to 350 degrees, microwave-safe up to 4 minutes, and dishwasher safe. The word *porcelain* is derived from the Middle French word for cowrie shells.

Earthenware is a clay-based porous ceramic that is fired at low temperatures and often glazed in vivid colors. A good choice for everyday use, it is oven-safe up to 350 degrees, microwave-safe up to 4 minutes, and dishwasher safe.

Stoneware is made of heavy nonporous clay fired at very high temperatures. It has a more textural, hand-crafted look and, like earthenware, is great for everyday use as well as less expensive than porcelain.

❧ A Registry Checklist

ITEM	DESCRIPTION	QUANTITY	STORE

Bakeware

ITEM	DESCRIPTION	QUANTITY	STORE
Bundt form pan			
Cookie sheet			
Loaf pan			
Muffin pan			
Pie pan			
Pizza brick			
Sheet pan			
Springform pan			
Other			

ITEM	DESCRIPTION	QUANTITY	STORE

Barware

ITEM	DESCRIPTION	QUANTITY	STORE
Beer mugs			
Coasters			
Corkscrew			
Highballs			

ITEM	DESCRIPTION	QUANTITY	STORE
Ice bucket/tongs	_____	_____	_____
Pilsners	_____	_____	_____
Pitcher	_____	_____	_____
Wine decanter	_____	_____	_____
Wine rack	_____	_____	_____
Other	_____	_____	_____
	_____	_____	_____
	_____	_____	_____

ITEM	DESCRIPTION	QUANTITY	STORE

Linens

	DESCRIPTION	QUANTITY	STORE
Bath sheets	_____	_____	_____
Bath towels	_____	_____	_____
Bedspreads	_____	_____	_____
Blankets	_____	_____	_____
Cloth napkins	_____	_____	_____
Comforter/duvet	_____	_____	_____
Formal napkins	_____	_____	_____
Formal tablecloths	_____	_____	_____
Hand towels	_____	_____	_____

ITEM	DESCRIPTION	QUANTITY	STORE
Place mats	_____	_____	_____
Sheets	_____	_____	_____
Shower curtain	_____	_____	_____
Washcloths	_____	_____	_____
Other	_____	_____	_____
	_____	_____	_____
	_____	_____	_____

ITEM	DESCRIPTION	QUANTITY	STORE

Crystal

ITEM	DESCRIPTION	QUANTITY	STORE
Brandy snifters	_____	_____	_____
Champagne flutes	_____	_____	_____
Cordials	_____	_____	_____
Decanters	_____	_____	_____
Goblets	_____	_____	_____
Pitchers	_____	_____	_____
Wineglasses	_____	_____	_____
Other	_____	_____	_____
	_____	_____	_____
	_____	_____	_____

ITEM	DESCRIPTION	QUANTITY	STORE
Cutlery			
Bread knife	_____	_____	_____
Chef's knives	_____	_____	_____
Cleaver	_____	_____	_____
Cutting board	_____	_____	_____
Kitchen shears	_____	_____	_____
Knife block	_____	_____	_____
Paring knife	_____	_____	_____
Sharpening tool	_____	_____	_____
Steak knives	_____	_____	_____
Other	_____	_____	_____
	_____	_____	_____
	_____	_____	_____

ITEM	DESCRIPTION	QUANTITY	STORE
Dinnerware			
Accent plates	_____	_____	_____
Bread and butter plates	_____	_____	_____
Buffet plates	_____	_____	_____
Cereal bowls	_____	_____	_____

ITEM	DESCRIPTION	QUANTITY	STORE
Coffee cups and saucers			
Dessert plates			
Dinner plates			
Egg cups			
Mugs			
Salad bowls			
Service plates			
Soup bowls			
Other			

ITEM	DESCRIPTION	QUANTITY	STORE

Electronics

Camera			
CD player			
Clock radio			
Computer			
Fax machine			
Television			

ITEM	DESCRIPTION	QUANTITY	STORE
Video camera			
VCR			
Other			

ITEM	DESCRIPTION	QUANTITY	STORE

Flatware

ITEM	DESCRIPTION	QUANTITY	STORE
Creamed soup spoons			
Soup spoons			
Dinner forks			
Dinner knives			
Salad/dessert forks			
Teaspoons			
Dessert spoons			
Other			

ITEM	DESCRIPTION	QUANTITY	STORE

Glassware

ITEM	DESCRIPTION	QUANTITY	STORE
Everyday glasses			
Juice glasses			

ITEM	DESCRIPTION	QUANTITY	STORE

Kitchen Linens

ITEM	DESCRIPTION	QUANTITY	STORE
Apron			
Dish cloths			
Dish towels			
Napkins			
Oven mitts			
Pot holders			
Tablecloths			

ITEM	DESCRIPTION	QUANTITY	STORE

Kitchenware

ITEM	DESCRIPTION	QUANTITY	STORE
Blender			
Breadmaker			
Coffeemaker			
Colander			

ITEM	DESCRIPTION	QUANTITY	STORE
Cookbooks			
Cook's spoon (slotted)			
Cook's spoon (solid)			
Cookware utensils			
Cooling rack			
Electric skillet			
Espresso/cappuccino maker			
Food processor			
Garlic press			
Grater			
Gravy/sauce ladle			
Hand mixer			
Ice cream maker			
Juicer			
Measuring set			
Microwave oven			
Mixing bowls			
Pasta machine			
Pie/cake server			
Pizza cutter			

ITEM	DESCRIPTION	QUANTITY	STORE
Popcorn popper			
Roasting pan			
Salad servers			
Saucepans			
Serving utensils			
Skillets			
Steamer			
Stock pots			
Teakettle			
Thermometer			
Timer			
Toaster			
Waffle iron			
Wok			
Other			

ITEM	DESCRIPTION	QUANTITY	STORE

Serving Pieces

ITEM	DESCRIPTION	QUANTITY	STORE
Bread tray	_____	_____	_____
Butter dish	_____	_____	_____
Cake plate	_____	_____	_____
Cream and sugar bowls	_____	_____	_____
Gravy boat	_____	_____	_____
Platters	_____	_____	_____
Salt and pepper shakers	_____	_____	_____
Other	_____	_____	_____
	_____	_____	_____
	_____	_____	_____

ITEM	DESCRIPTION	QUANTITY	STORE

Miscellaneous

ITEM	DESCRIPTION	QUANTITY	STORE
Barbecue	_____	_____	_____
Baskets	_____	_____	_____
Candlestick holders	_____	_____	_____
Exercise/ sporting equipment	_____	_____	_____
Furniture	_____	_____	_____
Luggage	_____	_____	_____

ITEM	DESCRIPTION	QUANTITY	STORE
Mirrors	_____	_____	_____
Picture frames	_____	_____	_____
Tools	_____	_____	_____
Vacuum cleaner	_____	_____	_____
Vases	_____	_____	_____
Other	_____	_____	_____
	_____	_____	_____
	_____	_____	_____

❧ *Stores Where Gifts Are Registered*

Store_____

Address_____

Registry consultant _____   Phone_____   Fax_____

Store_____

Address_____

Registry consultant _____   Phone_____   Fax_____

Store_____

Address_____

Registry consultant _____   Phone_____   Fax_____

From Glassware to Crystal

Consider your china, everyday dinnerware, and flatware patterns when choosing glassware and crystal. Have your registry consultant set up sample place settings so that you can see how everything looks together.

Because glass is breakable, you might want to register for more than the standard eight to twelve pieces of each item.

Glassware is made of sand mixed with natural elements. It's for everyday use (dishwasher safe) and includes everything from juice glasses to tall iced tea glasses.

Crystal is more delicate than ordinary glass but also heavier and more brilliant, with a clarity all its own. It is made from sand mixed with natural elements and 24 percent to 34 percent lead. Registry consultants classify crystal by its function as either barware (sherry glasses, brandy snifters, and high- and low-ball glasses) or stemware (water goblets, wineglasses, and champagne glasses for formal dining). Crystal is dishwasher safe as long as it is placed carefully and securely in the rack. When you wash it by hand, use a rubber mat on the sink's bottom to cushion the glass and a splash of ammonia to reduce spotting and maintain overall sparkle.

I f we haven't been totally clear, we'll state it succinctly now: Gifts are not just things bought and wrapped! You want to keep a record of all the giving those who love you will do during this special time, whether they are gifts of time such as prepared meals or dishes, heirloom items passed down to you, financial gifts, or good old-fashioned gift-wrapped presents.

Pay very careful attention to your Thank Yous. You will, of course, show appreciation for gifts in person and by phone, but even in those cases, a written note is a *must* for every material and financial gift, as well as every sacrifice of time. The aunt who "burns" in her kitchen to make you that special dish for your rehearsal dinner deserves a formal Thank You note just as much as the other aunt who got you the china from Tiffany. Be sure to order thank you notes (see chapter 10), and if you will not be able to get your notes out promptly, order acknowledgment cards.

One final word about Thank You notes and cards: The message is never printed on the inside of the card and no two should read exactly the same, even when you receive the same gift! There's no work sheet here, brothers and sisters, for Thank You cards, because each one needs to be its own heartfelt message.

As you use the work sheet that follows, coordinate it with your guest list in chapter 3, where you will have recorded all the addresses. While some planners combine the guest list and gifts list, we let them complement one another because of the expanded definition of gift-giving in communities of the African Diaspora. Remember, not every guest will give a gift of the boxed, wrapped variety. Think about the other-mother who gives you a check for the deposit on your reception site, passes down to you her heirloom gown, gets the Women's Guild at her church to cook and serve your rehearsal dinner, and shows up at the wedding with a box from your favorite department store. She deserves more than the single Thank You note you'd check off on your guest list. Using the separate gift record here will help you be thorough in your thanking.

❧ *Record of Gifts Received*

Gift Description	Given By	Where Purchased	Date Rec'd	Thank You
wooden salad bowl	Mr. & Mrs. W. Smith	Macy's	8/31/98	9/6/98
oxtails for 20 people	Almagen Sykes	home-cooked	9/15/98	9/22/98

GIFT DESCRIPTION	GIVEN BY	WHERE PURCHASED	DATE REC'D	THANK YOU

GIFT DESCRIPTION	GIVEN BY	WHERE PURCHASED	DATE REC'D	THANK YOU

GIFT DESCRIPTION	GIVEN BY	WHERE PURCHASED	DATE REC'D	THANK YOU

I n the midst of all this receiving, you'll also want to give. It's customary for the bride and groom to give gifts to the wedding party and for the two of you to give token gifts to each other's parents. It also doesn't hurt to give them to your own parents! Think of gifts that will have special meaning and make everyone feel they are part of your joyous celebration. And while all this giving and receiving is going on, don't forget the Source of all gifts and blessings.

❧ Bride's Record of Gifts to Give

	IDEAS	FINAL SELECTION	DATE GIVEN
Bride's attendants	_____	_____	_____
	_____		
	_____		
	_____		
	_____		
Bridegroom's attendants	_____	_____	_____
	_____		
	_____		
	_____		
	_____		

	IDEAS	FINAL SELECTION	DATE GIVEN
Mother of the bride	_____	_____	_____
	_____		
	_____		
	_____		
	_____		
Father of the bride	_____	_____	_____
	_____		
	_____		
	_____		
	_____		
Mother of the bridegroom	_____	_____	_____
	_____		
	_____		
	_____		
	_____		
Father of the bridegroom	_____	_____	_____
	_____		
	_____		
Others	_____	_____	_____
	_____		
	_____		

❦ *Groom's Record of Gifts to Give*

	IDEAS	FINAL SELECTION	DATE GIVEN
Bride's attendants	_____	_____	_____
	_____		
	_____		
	_____		
	_____		
Bridegroom's attendants	_____	_____	_____
	_____		
	_____		
	_____		
	_____		
Mother of the bride	_____	_____	_____
	_____		
	_____		
	_____		
	_____		
Father of the bride	_____	_____	_____
	_____		
	_____		
	_____		
	_____		

	IDEAS	FINAL SELECTION	DATE GIVEN
Mother of the bridegroom	_____	_____	_____
	_____		
	_____		
	_____		
	_____		
	_____		
	_____		
Father of the bridegroom	_____	_____	_____
	_____		
	_____		
	_____		
	_____		
Others	_____	_____	_____
	_____		
	_____		
	_____		
	_____		

. . . and all this partying is only the beginning . . .

Twelve

GOOD-BYE TO THE SINGLE LIFE:

PRE-WEDDING PARTIES

N THE MIDST of all the fun and excitement of planning

your wedding, you'll want to take some time to look back,

too, and treasure the wisdom and support of those who've

come this far with you and will be seeing you into the new life that lies ahead.

Bridal showers used to be sedate all-sister gatherings with gift-giving that focused on setting up the couple's new household—primarily with china, silver, and linens. And keeping or improvising on that tradition is just fine. But you and your groom may already have fully equipped households or your wish lists may be much more offbeat and personal. You might prefer to spend this precious transitional time receiving emotional and spiritual gifts to bring into your married lives. Let your own needs and desires—not the dictates of tradition—shape your pre-wedding festivities.

Today there are lots of options available to you to personalize the traditional shower. Pick something you love—bath accoutrements or bike gear—and center your shower and gifts around it. If you and your husband-to-be are decorating a new home, pick a room in the house and let friends equip it for you. If you quilt, garden, or do a craft, make that the theme of your shower. Perhaps you're passionate about a cause. Get all your friends to give a gift of a few hours of their time as your shower present, say, reading to kids or visiting the elderly in a nursing home. Such service showers provide a way for you to spread the love and joy of your impending marriage into the Black community and way beyond those attending the ceremony and reception.

When your family or sister-friends begin to plan your shower, let them know if you want to invite the guys. With or without the brothers, follow our ancestors' example and include the elders. Suggest that your friends throw you an African-inspired shower. Let the older women in your life share their marital wisdom in stories, poems, and verse, celebrating our rich oral tradition. Or, use the Kwanzaa principles (all or just ones special to you) as the basis for your sister-circle to provide handmade or Afrocentric gifts for you.

Whatever your shower preference, ask specifically for what you want, whether it is wares to help you fill your kitchen cupboards and linen closets or their time and thoughts to strengthen you as you prepare to fulfill the commitment you are about to make. Or both!

If you have different groups of friends—coworkers, fellow church members, sorority sisters—each may want you to celebrate with them. As long as you're sensitive to everybody's feelings and finances, there's no limit (except time) to the number and kind of showers you can attend.

Use the work sheets below to make it easier for those who love you to plan these celebrations. These work sheets can be a good record for you to remember who came to share your memories of single life and your hopes for the future and their words of love and wisdom.

❧ Shower Work Sheet

Shower #1

Hosts _____

Date and time _____

Place_____

Theme/style_____

Guest List

NAME	**ADDRESS**	**PHONE**
_____	_____	_____
_____	_____	_____
_____	_____	_____
_____	_____	_____
_____	_____	_____
_____	_____	_____
_____	_____	_____
_____	_____	_____
_____	_____	_____

Comments _____

_____

_____

_____

Shower #2

Hosts _____

Date and time _____

Place _____

Theme/style _____

Guest List

NAME	ADDRESS	PHONE

Comments _____

_____

_____

_____

The next form will help you keep track of the wonderful gifts you will receive and the Thank You notes you will send.

⮹ *Record of Shower Gifts Received and Thank You's Given*

NAME	ADDRESS	GIFT	THANK YOU NOTE

NAME	ADDRESS	GIFT	THANK YOU NOTE

Yₒu'll probably also want to spend some celebratory time before your wedding with those who'll be walking down the aisle with you—your attendants. If they don't already all know each other, this can be a good opportunity for introductions. It's also an appropriate time for you to show your appreciation for their help and support by giving them gifts.

Such parties can be given by the bridesmaids for you or by you for the bridesmaids. In either case, the work sheet below will help structure the planning.

❧ *Bridesmaids' Party Work Sheet*

Type of party _____   Date _____   Time _____

Hostess(es)   _____   _____

                           _____   _____

                           _____   _____

Address _____   Phone _____

Number of guests _____

Comments _____

_____

_____

_____

_____

_____

❧ *Guest List* ❧

YES/NO	**NAME**	**ADDRESS**	**PHONE**
__/__	_____	_____	_____
__/__	_____	_____	_____
__/__	_____	_____	_____
__/__	_____	_____	_____
__/__	_____	_____	_____
__/__	_____	_____	_____
__/__	_____	_____	_____
__/__	_____	_____	_____
__/__	_____	_____	_____
__/__	_____	_____	_____
__/__	_____	_____	_____
__/__	_____	_____	_____
__/__	_____	_____	_____
__/__	_____	_____	_____
__/__	_____	_____	_____
__/__	_____	_____	_____
__/__	_____	_____	_____
__/__	_____	_____	_____
__/__	_____	_____	_____

Total _____

Party Details

MENU & BEVERAGES	COST	DECORATIONS, RENTALS, ETC.	COST
_____	$ ____	_____	$ ____
_____	$ ____	_____	$ ____
_____	$ ____	_____	$ ____
_____	$ ____	_____	$ ____
_____	$ ____	_____	$ ____
_____	$ ____	_____	$ ____
_____	$ ____	_____	$ ____
_____	$ ____	_____	$ ____
_____	$ ____	_____	$ ____
_____	$ ____	_____	$ ____
_____	$ ____	_____	$ ____
_____	$ ____	_____	$ ____
_____	$ ____	_____	$ ____
_____	$ ____	_____	$ ____
_____	$ ____	_____	$ ____
_____	$ ____	_____	$ ____
_____	$ ____	_____	$ ____
_____	$ ____	_____	$ ____

Gratuity included Yes ❑ No ❑   Estimated cost per person $_____

The groom and his friends, relatives, and attendants get to celebrate before your wedding, too. In the past, their celebrations have sometimes been as wild as the bride's have been sedate. Even the traditional groomsmen's party took place at night, with dinner and drinks, while the bridesmaids usually had lunch with tea and sandwiches.

Today, your man need not follow tradition any more than you do. He may want to have special time with his brothers and elders, gathering their support and wisdom, or the two of you may decide to have your pre-wedding parties together. (And if he decides on a boyz night out, there's nothing to say you can't have a girls' night out!)

Encourage him to think about the form of celebration that would be most meaningful to him and to keep a record that he, too, can look back on in the years ahead.

❧ Bachelor Party Work Sheet

Type of party _____ Date _____ Time _____

Host _____ _____

_____ _____

_____ _____

Address _____ Phone _____

Number of guests _____

Comments _____

_____

_____

_____

_____

❧ *Guest List* ❧

R.S.V.P. YES/NO	NAME	ADDRESS	PHONE
__ / __			
__ / __			
__ / __			
__ / __			
__ / __			
__ / __			
__ / __			
__ / __			
__ / __			
__ / __			
__ / __			
__ / __			
__ / __			
__ / __			
__ / __			
__ / __			
__ / __			
__ / __			

Total _____

❦ *Party Details* ❧

MENU & BEVERAGES	COST	DECORATIONS, RENTALS, ETC.	COST
_____	$ _____	_____	$ _____
_____	$ _____	_____	$ _____
_____	$ _____	_____	$ _____
_____	$ _____	_____	$ _____
_____	$ _____	_____	$ _____
_____	$ _____	_____	$ _____
_____	$ _____	_____	$ _____
_____	$ _____	_____	$ _____
_____	$ _____	_____	$ _____
_____	$ _____	_____	$ _____
_____	$ _____	_____	$ _____
_____	$ _____	_____	$ _____
_____	$ _____	_____	$ _____
_____	$ _____	_____	$ _____
_____	$ _____	_____	$ _____
_____	$ _____	_____	$ _____
_____	$ _____	_____	$ _____

Gratuity included Yes ❑   No ❑   Estimated cost per person $_____

As mentioned earlier, you might just want to party. Toss all the boy-girl stuff to the wind and just let your friends celebrate you. Or do your own version of a Queh-Queh, a Guyanese coed drumming, song, and dance celebration usually held two weeks before the wedding. Make it easy on everyone by using this work sheet.

❧ Pre-wedding Party Work Sheet

Type of party _____ Date_____ Time_____

Host(s) _____ _____

_____ _____

_____ _____

Address _____ Phone_____

Number of guests _____

Comments _____

_____

_____

_____

_____

_____

_____

Guest List

R.S.V.P. Yes/No	Name	Address	Phone
__/__			
__/__			
__/__			
__/__			
__/__			
__/__			
__/__			
__/__			
__/__			
__/__			
__/__			
__/__			
__/__			
__/__			
__/__			
__/__			
__/__			
__/__			

Total ______

MENU & BEVERAGES	COST	DECORATIONS, RENTALS, ETC.	COST
_____	$ _____	_____	$ _____
_____	$ _____	_____	$ _____
_____	$ _____	_____	$ _____
_____	$ _____	_____	$ _____
_____	$ _____	_____	$ _____
_____	$ _____	_____	$ _____
_____	$ _____	_____	$ _____
_____	$ _____	_____	$ _____
_____	$ _____	_____	$ _____
_____	$ _____	_____	$ _____
_____	$ _____	_____	$ _____
_____	$ _____	_____	$ _____
_____	$ _____	_____	$ _____
_____	$ _____	_____	$ _____
_____	$ _____	_____	$ _____
_____	$ _____	_____	$ _____
_____	$ _____	_____	$ _____
_____	$ _____	_____	$ _____

Gratuity included Yes ☐ No ☐

Estimated cost per person $_____

You say, "I want to be my most beautiful on my wedding day." And in the years to come, he'll kiss your face and say, "You are most beautiful to me today."

Thirteen

KEEPING YOURSELF TOGETHER:

FITNESS, HEALTH, AND BEAUTY

OUR WEDDING DAY is going to be one of the most beautiful days of your life. So while you're planning the where, what, and who, plan the you. Prepare for your figure to look "slammin." Make sure you are glowing with health. Indulge yourself in some luxury beauty care so you appear resplendent. And set aside some time in advance to rest so you look and feel refreshed on that Big Day. In this chapter we give you some planning tools to help you look and feel your best.

The last thing you need amid all your other tasks two weeks before your wedding is to start counting calories or dieting. If you decide to lose weight for your Big Day, the time we recommend you begin that program (and most doctors agree with us) is the same time we recommend you begin your wedding planning: twelve to eighteen months before the nuptial date. Use the Pre-wedding Food Diary below to plan your menus and curb any tendencies to overindulge. (Photocopy it for as many weeks as you need.)

❧ *Pre-wedding Food Diary*

Week #1

	M	T	W	TH	FR	SAT	SUN
Breakfast	___	___	___	___	___	___	___
	___	___	___	___	___	___	___
	___	___	___	___	___	___	___
	___	___	___	___	___	___	___
	___	___	___	___	___	___	___
Snack	___	___	___	___	___	___	___
	___	___	___	___	___	___	___
Lunch	___	___	___	___	___	___	___
	___	___	___	___	___	___	___
	___	___	___	___	___	___	___
	___	___	___	___	___	___	___

	M	**T**	**W**	**Th**	**Fr**	**Sat**	**Sun**
Snack	_____	_____	_____	_____	_____	_____	_____
	_____	_____	_____	_____	_____	_____	_____
Dinner	_____	_____	_____	_____	_____	_____	_____
	_____	_____	_____	_____	_____	_____	_____
	_____	_____	_____	_____	_____	_____	_____
	_____	_____	_____	_____	_____	_____	_____
	_____	_____	_____	_____	_____	_____	_____
Other	_____	_____	_____	_____	_____	_____	_____
	_____	_____	_____	_____	_____	_____	_____
	_____	_____	_____	_____	_____	_____	_____
	_____	_____	_____	_____	_____	_____	_____
	_____	_____	_____	_____	_____	_____	_____

Week #2

	M	**T**	**W**	**Th**	**Fr**	**Sat**	**Sun**
Breakfast	_____	_____	_____	_____	_____	_____	_____
	_____	_____	_____	_____	_____	_____	_____
	_____	_____	_____	_____	_____	_____	_____
	_____	_____	_____	_____	_____	_____	_____
	_____	_____	_____	_____	_____	_____	_____

	M	T	W	Th	Fr	Sat	Sun
Snack	_____	_____	_____	_____	_____	_____	_____
	_____	_____	_____	_____	_____	_____	_____
Lunch	_____	_____	_____	_____	_____	_____	_____
	_____	_____	_____	_____	_____	_____	_____
	_____	_____	_____	_____	_____	_____	_____
	_____	_____	_____	_____	_____	_____	_____
Snack	_____	_____	_____	_____	_____	_____	_____
	_____	_____	_____	_____	_____	_____	_____
Dinner	_____	_____	_____	_____	_____	_____	_____
	_____	_____	_____	_____	_____	_____	_____
	_____	_____	_____	_____	_____	_____	_____
	_____	_____	_____	_____	_____	_____	_____
Other	_____	_____	_____	_____	_____	_____	_____
	_____	_____	_____	_____	_____	_____	_____
	_____	_____	_____	_____	_____	_____	_____
	_____	_____	_____	_____	_____	_____	_____

Don't skip this section, Ms. Almost-Married. Unlike dieting, gentle exercise, like walking, is a good thing to begin anytime. (Of course, check with your doctor before you begin any strenuous or new exercise program.) Plan a brisk walk, a swim, bicycling, dance, a gym workout, or whatever exercise you enjoy at least three times each week. And, as an extra motivator, a recent study showed men thought physical fitness was the best indicator of good sexual performance in women. Take the tip!

Photocopy the following exercise worksheet to keep you on track. The time is now for beginning an exercise plan. If you haven't been exercising, start slowly. Don't attempt to start a rigorous training regime a week before the wedding. The last thing you need is to be sore on your big day.

❧ Pre-wedding Exercise Plan

Week #1

	DAY	**DATE**	**TIME**	**ACTIVITY**
First exercise	_____	/_____	/_____	_____
Second exercise	_____	/_____	/_____	_____
Third exercise	_____	/_____	/_____	_____

Week #2

	DAY	**DATE**	**TIME**	**ACTIVITY**
First exercise	_____	/_____	/_____	_____
Second exercise	_____	/_____	/_____	_____
Third exercise	_____	/_____	/_____	_____

Week #3

	DAY	DATE	TIME	ACTIVITY
First exercise	____	/____	/____	_____
Second exercise	____	/____	/____	_____
Third exercise	____	/____	/____	_____

THE MANE EVENT

Braids, perms, hot presses, weaves, locks, china balls, twists, almost-shaves—we women of African descent run the gamut of hair acts, and it's all good. You choose your style, and we'll help you keep it beautiful for your wedding day. It's all about planning and common sense.

Do plan a visit to your stylist for a consultation for your wedding "do." You and she know how your hair behaves. Schedule accordingly. If it looks best the day it's done then you may want your stylist on site the morning of the wedding to do your hair before you dress. If it looks its best a day or so after it's done, when the style has had time to rest, then go in for your appointment a few days prior to the Big Day.

Do what you know works for your hair. But pay attention to these few don'ts: don't switch stylists just before the wedding; don't try a new style for the first time just before, either; don't choose a style that will shock your man as you walk down the aisle or one that will make him feel you are uncuddleable during your honeymoon.

Use the form below to make sure you plan that important appointment with your stylist.

❧ Hairstyle Work Sheet

Salon _____

Address _____

Stylist _____

Hair texture _____

Color_____ Style_____

Cut_____ Perm_____

Appointment date _____ Time_____

Cost $ _____

GETTING THAT GLOW

Most of us pay attention to our hair, but fewer of us really focus on our skin. But in another survey, when brothers were asked what they most liked about us Black women physically, the highest response was . . . no, not our behinds. They most like our skin. Will we ever figure them out?

Plan to spend an hour at a good makeup counter where you can get plenty of skin-care advice, and use this work sheet to start taking better care of your body's biggest organ, your skin.

❧ *Skin-care Work Sheet*

Skin type _____

Cleanser_____

Toner _____

Exfoliation cream _____

Hydrator/moisturizer _____

Mask_____

Other _____

_____

A generation ago, makeup for women of color was a big challenge. Today, the challenge is choosing from the overabundance of options. Pay special attention to your makeup for your Big Day, as it presents some concerns you might not normally encounter. You need to be camera-ready, which means more makeup, especially powder (to fight oiliness and shine), but you also need to be most huggable and kissable, which means less makeup. Plan your makeup routine for the day with a good over-the-counter makeup advisor or by hiring a makeup artist. Test your makeup several weeks before the wedding. Use this work sheet to record what works, so you can repeat it on the Big Day.

❧ *Cosmetics for Women of Color* ❧

The following companies either have separate lines that are specifically geared to women of color or lines that include shades for them:

- ❧ **Avon's Tones of Beauty**
- ❧ **Cover Girl**
- ❧ **Iman Cosmetics**
- ❧ **Estée Lauder**
- ❧ **L'Oreal**
- ❧ **Mary Kay Cosmetics**
- ❧ **Maybelline's Shades of You**
- ❧ **Patti LaBelle Cosmetics**
- ❧ **Revlon's Colorstyle Collection**
- ❧ **Prescriptives**

🐦 Makeup Chart

PRODUCT	COLOR	PLACEMENT
_____	_____	_____
_____	_____	_____
_____	_____	_____
_____	_____	_____
_____	_____	_____
_____	_____	_____
_____	_____	_____
_____	_____	_____
_____	_____	_____

If you use a makeup artist, get a contract. Don't skip it; trust us. While you're hiring someone to do your makeup, arrange for her to do your mother and your attendants. They'll love you for it. Ask him to put a dash of powder on your groom's forehead, too. If your man balks, remind him of that much-joked-about shiny forehead in those old family wedding portraits.

🐦 Makeup Artist's Contract Work Sheet

Artist _____

Assistant's name_____

Address _____

Phone_____ Fax _____

Date _____ Location _____

Arrival time _____

Cost of the bride's makeup $_____

Additional costs $ _____

Bridesmaids _____yes _____no $ _____cost

Mother of the bride _____yes _____no $ _____cost

Bridegroom _____yes _____no $ _____cost

Groomsmen _____yes _____no $ _____cost

Who supplies makeup _____

Artist's transportation _____

Schedule_____

Total Cost $ _____

Terms of payment _____ _____

Deposit date _____ Amount of deposit $_____

Balance due _____ Amount of balance $_____

HAND CARE

On no other day will your hands be so squeezed, so held, so photographed. Need we say more? Start softening them a few weeks before the wedding and schedule that manicure. Go ahead and splurge for a pedicure while you're at it.

❧ Manicure Work Sheet

Salon _____

Address _____

Manicurist _____

Nail color _____ Extras _____

Appointment date _____ Time _____

Cost $ _____

❧ Hand Care Work Sheet

	PRODUCT NAME	MANUFACTURER
Moisturizer	_____	_____
Other products	_____	_____

KEEPING YOUR COOL

Even great joy is stressful. Take time now to write down the words that will calm you in those last days of single life, as your wedding day approaches. Perhaps those words are prayers, passages from your favorite books, Bible verses, or phrases from cards and notes you've received from loved ones.

✎ *Affirmations* ✎

_____

_____

_____

_____

_____

_____

_____

_____

_____

_____

_____

_____

_____

_____

_____

_____

_____

_____

_____

_____

_____

Affirmations are terrific. They ease the mind and, studies show, they also affect the body. But if you can spare the time and expense, give your body some special treatment of its own. Plan a trip to a day spa, get a massage, treat yourself to a body waxing, or try one of the many new pampering treatments offered at spas today. (Or even plan a couple's day, so you can chill out together!)

✎ Break-Day Beauty Schedule

TIME	PLACE	TREATMENT	CONTACT/ADDRESS/PHONE
____	_____	_____	_____
____	_____	_____	_____
____	_____	_____	_____
____	_____	_____	_____
____	_____	_____	_____
____	_____	_____	_____
____	_____	_____	_____
____	_____	_____	_____
____	_____	_____	_____

YOUR BEAUTIFUL SELF ON YOUR WEDDING DAY

Here's a work sheet to make sure all the activities that will make you your most beautiful happen smoothly. You don't want the makeup artist tripping over the stylist. And, if you're doing all this yourself, you don't want to forget any element of your personal care if you're interrupted by having to attend to last-minute details.

✎ *Wedding Day Beauty Schedule* ✎

TIME	PLACE	TASK	CONTACT

TIME	PLACE	TASK	CONTACT
____	_____	_____	_____
____	_____	_____	_____
____	_____	_____	_____
____	_____	_____	_____
____	_____	_____	_____
____	_____	_____	_____
____	_____	_____	_____

Remember, beauty ultimately comes from within. It's the love that flows from your heart that will make every inch of you gorgeous.

Just the way they always imagined it would be.
This couple begins their "happily ever after" at Club Jamaica Beach Resort.

Fourteen

PLANNING YOUR HONEYMOON

HE TWO OF YOU awake to the sound of the sea gently lapping at the beach right outside the door to your guest cottage. No phone calls to make, no deliveries to receive, no list of things to do. Maybe you'll even skip the sightseeing today and just stay right where you are . . . in each other's arms. With careful planning, your honeymoon can be the intimate time together you've always dreamed of, the romantic beginning of your married life.

Just as you and your fiancé envisioned your dream wedding in chapter I, sit down together, soon after you've set your ceremony date, to envision your dream honeymoon. Ask each other the questions below and write down your answers separately:

❧ *Honeymoon Questionnaire*

❧ *Bride's Vision* ❧

What is the most romantic setting you can imagine? _____

_____

_____

What do you most enjoy doing in your spare time? _____

_____

_____

What is your idea of the perfect time alone with your spouse? _____

_____

_____

⟊ *Bridegroom's Vision* ⟋

What is the most romantic setting you can imagine? _____

_____

_____

What do you most enjoy doing in your spare time? _____

_____

_____

What is your idea of the perfect time alone with your spouse? _____

_____

_____

When you compare your answers, you may be surprised to discover that you aren't in complete agreement. One of you may think that two weeks hiking in the wilderness is the ideal way to be alone with your most cherished companion. The other's idea of camping out might be a long weekend in a luxurious hotel with room service as your only contact with the outside world.

It's not unusual for highly compatible couples to have such divergent tastes, even different definitions of romance. Work together to compile a list of possible destinations that will satisfy both of your visions, and record them on the Destinations Work Sheet.

Keep in mind the time of year you're planning to marry and the popularity of the locations you're considering, as well as the length of your stay. If you choose a destination in the peak seasons, you can expect to pay peak prices, and you'll need to make your reservations months—even a year or more—in advance.

Consult guidebooks of the areas you're interested in at your local library or bookstore. The more prepared you are when you do talk to a travel agent, the more helpful the agent can be (and the more certain you can be that you're getting a good deal from an informed source).

The Perfect Destination

For many couples, sun and sea are the elements that conjure up the ultimate in romance as well as relaxation. The most popular honeymoon spots, according to the Association of Bridal Consultants, have plenty of both: Most newlyweds head to Florida, Hawaii, or the Caribbean Islands. We'll show you some of the highlights of these destinations and the reasons for their popularity, as well as offer some suggestions of other, lesser known places—far and near—that may expand your notions of "romantic."

Florida

From flashy Miami Beach to wholesome Walt Disney World to the coral reefs of the Keys—from spectacular wildlife to exciting nightlife—Florida has something for everyone. In a state with such a large tourist industry, it's possible to find lodging, food, and entertainment to fit any budget. Many hotels and resorts offer honeymoon packages. Air fares, especially from the Northeast, are extremely competitive.

Fort Lauderdale, with the ocean on one side, the Everglades on the other, and more than 300 navigable miles of inland waterways in between, an average temperature of 77 degrees, and 3,000 annual hours of sunshine, combines many of the natural attractions of the state as a whole. It has also been a leader in recognizing African-American contributions to its history and culture.

The Greater Fort Lauderdale Convention and Visitors Bureau publishes *The Visitors Guide to African-American Lifestyle and Culture,* which provides information on sports, shopping, restaurants, and nightlife of interest to Black tourists. Scuba dive or snorkel among the vast underwater wonderland of the area's natural and man-made reefs. Cut a swath through the reeds on an airboat ride through the Everglades. Take the Black Heritage Tour of the city's historic sites, which includes lunch at an African-American- or Caribbean-owned restaurant. Watch the yachts pull up to the Hyatt Regency Pier as you enjoy a late afternoon break. After dinner, dance the night away in one of the myriad clubs and discos.

Hawaii

Hawaii is America's most exotic state and most popular honeymoon destination. It has 132 islands and coral reefs stretching across 1,600 miles of ocean, and a native Polynesian population. Six major islands, each with a personality of its own, comprise Hawaii as we know it. Oahu, Maui, Hawaii, and Kauai are the most popular. Tiny Molokai is gaining favor as a get-away-from-it-all retreat. Lanai, once a plantation island almost totally owned by Dole Pineapple Company, has also become a tourist area. Easily reached from the Western United States, Hawaii is a honeymoon paradise for sun-and-sea-loving couples who are also in search of a culture and landscape different from their own but not quite foreign. The biggest challenge you face will be to decide which island or islands to visit on your trip, since you won't have time to see them all.

The Caribbean

More than thirty island nations, four languages, many more dialects, and African, European, Aboriginal, and Latin influences make up the delicious stew called the Caribbean. Combined with a year-round tropical climate and picture postcard scenery, this rich variety makes the Caribbean a destination to fit the bill of almost any honeymoon couple's ideal getaway.

The region's diversity and proximity to the United States offer a rare opportunity to experience several cultures during the course of a one- or two-week trip. From the East Coast, you can reach even the farthest Caribbean destination by air within four hours. Many visitors travel by cruise ships that make multiple ports of call.

❧ *Destinations Work Sheet*

LIST OF POSSIBLE DESTINATIONS	NOTES AND COMMENTS
1._____	_____
2._____	_____
3._____	_____
4._____	_____

MAKING THE ARRANGEMENTS

Once you've made a list of possible destinations that suit your dream, your budget, and your schedule, you're ready to compile a list of questions for your travel agent. (If you decide to book your honeymoon yourselves, rather than through an agent, remember that researching the deals available can be very time-consuming, although many destinations and most airlines now have Internet sites that can be very helpful.)

Here's a sample list of questions to ask.

❧ *Questionnaire for Your Travel Agent* ❧

Have you had experience sending other clients to our destination(s)? _____

What are the options for transportation to and from, and the costs? _____

_____

_____

Can we save by booking well in advance? _____

Will we need additional transportation (a rental car, for instance) at the destination? _____

_____

_____

_____

What are the choices for accommodation, and which would you recommend? Are there packages or all-

inclusive resorts we should consider? What exactly do they include? Are there any hidden costs we

should plan for? _____

_____

_____

_____

_____

Do we need any special documents for traveling? Any immunizations? How much time should we allow

for these? _____

_____

_____

Do you recommend travel insurance for this destination? _____

What is the currency and exchange rate? Should we get traveler's checks, or can we just use credit cards?

_____

_____

Are there any entrance fees or departure taxes? _____

What kind of weather can we expect at the time of year we're traveling? Can we take advantage of off-

season rates? _____

_____

_____

What are the guidelines for tipping for the services we receive as we travel? _____

_____

_____

When do we need to make our reservations, and what are the terms of payment? _____

_____

_____

Can we get written confirmation of our arrangements? _____

_____

_____

When you call or visit your agent, first read her a copy of your dream honeymoon description, share your list of destinations, and tell her your budget. She may have suggestions of other places that would fit your ideal or special honeymoon packages.

As you gather information for possible destinations, record it in the following work sheets for easy reference and comparison.

A Trip to the Motherland

Maybe you're looking for a place to spend your honeymoon that will bring you closer to your origins, that will celebrate your union with each other as well as with those who have gone before you, that will link your lives with your ancestors. Africa—especially the horn of West Africa—is just starting to become a popular destination for Black honeymooners.

Ghana

The picturesque Republic of Ghana lies on the west coast of Africa between Togo and the Ivory Coast. Ghana derives its postindependence name from an ancient, powerful kingdom. The splendor of the past remains alive today in the religious royalty of the village chiefs, the magnificent works of art in gold, bronze, wood, and stone, and the ceremonial rhythms of life in towns, marketplaces, and fishing ports, from the rocky headlands and sandy bays of the capital city, Accra, to the beaches along the coastline to the south and the grasslands to the north. Ghana is a tropical haven waiting to be explored.

Senegal

Just seven hours by plane from New York City, Senegal is a young, modern democracy with a long history of welcoming other cultures while preserving its own. Once part of the great West African Empires of Mali, Ghana, and Tekrur, Senegal has retained a sense of pageantry that is still visible in its everyday life. Its French-speaking and largely Muslim inhabitants are noted for their hospitality and friendliness. With its 350 miles of fine, sandy beaches, its national parks and wildlife preserves, its historic sites and crafts, and its world-renowned sport fishing and big game hunting, Senegal offers travelers a wide variety of scenery and activities.

Budget $_____

Tentative dates of travel: From   _____   to   _____

Plan #1

Agency _____   Agent _____

Address _____

Phone _____   Fax _____

Destination(s) _____

Document requirements _____

Amount of days _____   Reservation deadline _____

Transportation (air, ship, rail, bus, car)

Airport limousine $ _____

Rental cars $ _____

Gas $ _____

Tolls $ _____

Departure taxes $ _____

Taxis $ _____

Total cost $ _____

Accommodations (hotels, resorts, guest houses, inns)

Room rate (per day) $ _____

Taxes/surcharges $ _____

Tips & gratuities $ _____

Other services $ _____

Total cost $ _____

Meal plans (American plan, Modified American plan, European plan, Continental breakfast)

Breakfast $ _____

Lunch $ _____

Dinner $ _____

Snacks $ _____

Gratuities $ _____

Total cost $ _____

Entertainment

Sight-seeing/tours $ _____

Nightclubs/discos $ _____

Golf $ _____

Total cost $ _____

Purchases

Gifts/souvenirs $ _____

Grand total $ _____

Plan #2

Agency _____   Agent _____

Address _____

Phone_____   Fax _____

Destination(s) _____

Document requirements _____

Amount of days _____   Reservation deadline _____

Transportation (air, ship, rail, bus, car)

Airport limousine $ _____

Rental cars $ _____

Gas $ _____

Tolls $ _____

Departure taxes $ _____

Taxis $ _____

Total cost $ _____

Accommodations (hotels, resorts, guest houses, inns)

Room rate (per day) $ _____

Taxes/surcharges $ _____

Tips & gratuities $ _____

Other services $ _____

Total cost $ _____

Meal plans (American plan, modified American plan, European plan, Continental breakfast)

Breakfast $_____

Lunch $_____

Dinner $ _____

Snacks $ _____

Gratuities $_____

Total cost $ _____

Entertainment

Sight-seeing/tours $ _____

Nightclubs/discos $_____

Golf $_____

Total cost $ _____

Purchases

Gifts/souvenirs $_____

Grand total $_____

Plan #3

Agency _____   Agent _____

Address _____

Phone _____   Fax _____

Destination(s) _____

Document requirements _____

Amount of days _____   Reservation deadline _____

Transportation (air, ship, rail, bus, car)

Airport limousine $ _____

Rental cars $ _____

Gas $ _____

Tolls $ _____

Departure taxes $ _____

Taxis $ _____

Total cost $ _____

Accommodations (hotels, resorts, guest houses, inns)

Room rate (per day) $ _____

Taxes/surcharges $ _____

Tips & gratuities $ _____

Other services $ _____

Total cost $ _____

Meal plans (American plan, modified American plan, European plan, Continental breakfast)

Breakfast $ _____

Lunch $ _____

Dinner $ _____

Snacks $ _____

Gratuities $ _____

Total cost $ _____

Entertainment

Sight-seeing/tours $ _____

Nightclubs/discos $_____

Golf $ _____

Total cost $ _____

Purchases

Gifts/souvenirs $_____

Grand total $_____

After you've made your final decision, record all the details in the Booking Work Sheet below, and start the process for getting any necessary travel documents and immunizations. About two weeks before departure, pick up your tickets, written confirmation of your other reservations, and your itinerary from your agent and purchase traveler's checks if you're going to be using them. (Be sure to inform your bank if you're going to be withdrawing large sums of money. Some have security systems that will automatically close an account.)

❧ *Booking Work Sheet*

Agency_____   Agent _____

Address _____

Phone_____   Fax _____

Destination(s) _____

Transportation reservation_____

Hotel _____

Address _____

Phone_____   Fax _____

Accommodations _____

      Room rate $_____

Meal plan _____

Requirements_____

Reservations _____

      Departure date_____   Return date_____

      Reservations confirmed _____

Total cost $_____

      Deposit due $ _____   Date due_____

      Balance due $_____   Date balance due_____

Date to pick up tickets _____

Traveler's checks _____

      Bank _____

      Numbers _____

      _____

Papers and documents required

	BRIDE	GROOM		BRIDE	GROOM
International driver's license	❏	❏	Marriage license	❏	❏
Passport	❏	❏	Visa	❏	❏
Birth certificate	❏	❏	Inoculations needed	❏	❏
Airline tickets	❏	❏	Copies of prescriptions	❏	❏

Eight Safety Tips for Traveling

1. Make copies of your tickets, travel documents, traveler's checks, hotel reservations, and itineraries, record the numbers of your credit cards and bank cards, and pack them separately from the originals. Leave another copy with a friend at home.

2. Don't put all of your tickets and documents in one purse or pocket.

3. Carry only a minimum amount of cash at any time.

4. Lock your valuables in the hotel safe.

5. Always use the sliding lock or deadbolt when you're in your hotel room.

6. Don't leave your hotel keys in view while you're swimming, dining, or relaxing.

7. Always put luggage, packages, cameras, and other valuables in the trunk of your car.

8. Ask the staff of your hotel if there are any areas to avoid in the locality you are staying in.

COUNTDOWN TO TAKEOFF

To avoid last-minute additions to your already full pre-wedding schedule, use the Packing Checklist to plan your honeymoon wardrobe well in advance.

Traditionally, the bride inaugurates a new outfit for her getaway and some new lingerie (at least) for her wedding night. As soon as you've made your reservations, start thinking about ways you can heat up the bedroom climate, wherever you're headed.

Pack a few days before your wedding so that you have time to adjust for second thoughts and can make sure that your luggage is manageable. The usual impulse is to take too much, so try to control yourself when it comes to that third dinner dress or fourth bathing suit. You'll be glad not to have to struggle with all of those bags at the airport.

❧ Packing Checklist

	HERS	HIS
Casual sport clothes	_____	_____
	_____	_____
	_____	_____
	_____	_____
	_____	_____
Evening wear	_____	_____
	_____	_____
	_____	_____
	_____	_____
	_____	_____
Lingerie/underwear	_____	_____
	_____	_____
	_____	_____
	_____	_____
	_____	_____
Shoes/slippers	_____	_____
	_____	_____
	_____	_____

	HERS	**HIS**
Toiletries	_____	_____
	_____	_____
	_____	_____
	_____	_____
	_____	_____

Personal items/other:

	HERS	**HIS**
Camera	_____	_____
Credit card	_____	_____
Guidebooks	_____	_____
Passport	_____	_____
Tickets	_____	_____
Traveler's checks	_____	_____
Video camera	_____	_____

Bon voyage!

Paste a photo of your favorite honeymoon moment here.

After all the planning, partying, celebrating, and honeymooning, it's just the two of you. Ahhhh, at last. . . .

Fifteen

HAPPILY EVER AFTER

YOU'RE HOME FROM your honeymoon and the fond memories of your wedding day and romantic getaway still linger. Before life gets too busy, record your special thoughts here. You'll be glad you did when you leaf through these pages after your first spat or as you celebrate your golden anniversary fifty years from now.

Wedding Day and Honeymoon Memories

_____

_____

_____

_____

_____

_____

_____

_____

_____

_____

_____

_____

_____

_____

_____

_____

_____

_____

If you're like most couples, that first year of marriage will fly by, full of new surprises and lots of special firsts. You're probably contemplating a quiet First Anniversary celebration (just the two of you) or perhaps family and friends want to give you an anniversary party. If that is the case and you are the traditionalist who saved the top tier of your wedding cake, this is the day to remove it from the freezer and the box you preserved it in to share with those you love. Whatever you decide, be sure to record how your day was spent and with whom.

❧ Our First Anniversary

___

Traditional Gifts for Wedding Anniversaries

1st	paper
2nd	cotton
3rd	leather
4th	linen
5th	wood
6th	iron
7th	wool
8th	bronze
9th	pottery
10th	tin
11th	steel
12th	silk
13th	lace
14th	ivory
15th	crystal
16th	china
17th	silver
18th	pearls
19th	coral
20th	rubies
25th	sapphires
30th	gold
35th	emeralds
40th	diamonds

❧ *Record of Gifts Received on Our First Anniversary*

FROM	DATE RECEIVED	ITEM	DATE NOTE SENT

Happy anniversary from all of us at *Signature Bride* and we wish you many, many more! We know that while weddings celebrate the act of marriage, the real reason for the planning, the ritual, and the hooplah is to prepare our hearts for the joy that is daily life in union with a beloved companion. Live together long and well.

Photo Credits

Photos pages xviii, 110, 246, 320: Courtesy of Reginald Payton of Payton Studios.

Photos pages 4, 14, 164, 244: Courtesy of Dorothy Shi of Dorothy Shi Photography.

Photo page 42: Courtesy of The Philip Lief Group, photography by David Kelly Crow.

Photos pages 82, 88, 91 : Gowns by Alfred Angelo, gloves from Alfred Angelo glove collection.

Photo page 85: Courtesy of Nigerian Fabrics and Fashions; photography by Anderson Ballantyne, Brooklyn, NY; flowers by Ethnically Yours, Brooklyn, NY; accessories by Cellestine Collection, Brooklyn, NY.

Photos pages 118, 193: Courtesy of Garrett's Photography and Video.

Photos pages 133, 235: Courtesy of Tony Rose Studios.

Photos pages 200, 223: Courtesy of Polly Schoonmaker of Polly's Cakes, Portland, OR.

Photo page 228: Courtesy of James Spada of Spada Photography.

Photo page 258: Afrocentric invitation courtesy of Invitations by Dawn® mail order catalog.

Photo page 278: Courtesy of Carson Pirie Scott.

Photo page 304: Courtesy of Qualatex® balloons.

Photo page 336: © Ron Chapple, courtesy of Club Jamaica Beach Resort/Christine Valdes.

Photo page 356: Courtesy of the Greater Fort Lauderdale Convention and Visitors Bureau.